An Introduction to
Pastoral Counselling

By the same author

EVANGELICALS IN ACTION (*Bles*)
CHRISTIANS AND SOCIAL WORK (*S.C.M. Press*)
ARMY OF THE CHURCH (*Lutterworth*)

Kathleen Heasman, Ph.D.

LECTURER IN SOCIAL STUDIES
QUEEN ELIZABETH COLLEGE, LONDON UNIVERSITY

AN INTRODUCTION TO PASTORAL COUNSELLING

*For social workers,
the clergy, and others*

Constable London

First published in 1969
by Constable & Co Ltd
10 Orange Street, London WC2
Copyright © 1969 by Kathleen Heasman
All rights reserved

SBN 09 455770 5

253.5
H351

175579

Set in 12 on 14 pt Monotype Bembo
Printed in Great Britain
by The Anchor Press Ltd and bound by
Wm. Brendon & Son Ltd, both of Tiptree, Essex

Acknowledgments

Acknowledgments are due to Miss Helen Roberts, O.B.E., and to the Reverend Professor G. R. Dunstan for their initial encouragement in urging me to write this book; also to those who so kindly read through the manuscript and made many suggestions and comments – among them the Reverend William Kyle of the Methodist Counselling Centre, the Reverend Jack Smith of the Church Army Counselling Centre and Dr Alfred Torrie. Dr Walter B. Freed, of the Church of the Reformation, Rochester, New York State, has given me the benefit of his wide knowledge of American counselling methods; although the interpretation of these methods is my own. As usual, I am greatly indebted to Miss Vera Bowen for her faultless typing, and to Mrs Margaret Atkins, the Librarian of Queen Elizabeth College, for her unremitting efforts in making it possible for me to consult many of the less easily obtainable sources.

K.J.H.

Contents

	Preface	page ix
I	Society and Counselling	1
II	Persons in Relationship	20
III	A New Understanding of People	35
IV	The Basic Principles of Counselling	54
V	Counselling in Action	69
VI	The Pastoral Counsellor	92
VII	The Stages of the Human Life Span	110
	Counselling the Young	119
	Marriage Counselling	129
	Counselling the Middle-aged	137
	Counselling the Elderly	146
VIII	Counselling and Healing	157
	Counselling the Sick	161
	The Mentally Ill	171
	The Lonely and Inadequate	177
	Alcoholics and Drug Addicts	184
IX	Counselling in Groups	198
X	The Pastoral Approach	208
	References	216
	Bibliography	217
	Index	223

Preface

Pastoral counselling is frequently thought of in terms of the pastoral ministry of the clergy, or of those who hold some special position in relation to the spiritual needs of the individual. It assumes that the pastoral counsellor carries on his work within a defined institution – the church – and that he, therefore, has spiritual and sacramental resources which are not necessarily available to other counsellors.

A somewhat different interpretation of pastoral counselling is used in this book. Here pastoral counselling is regarded as a form of the normal process of social counselling, but one which takes into account the tripartite nature of man – his body, mind and spirit – and which seeks to help a person to reach a balance between these different aspects of his nature. Thus there is a difference between the pastoral care which a minister of religion has to offer, and pastoral counselling which he or any other suitably trained person may engage in. As a counsellor, the minister of religion will follow the general principles and methods of counselling used by everyone engaged in this way of helping other people. But in his ministerial capacity he will be able to add any spiritual or sacramental aids which his church has to offer. In many cases he will act solely as a pastoral counsellor without any reference to his religious identification. He may, of course, mingle pastoral care with pastoral counselling and then he is acting both as a pastoral counsellor and as one concerned as well with pastoral care. Or he may make some distinction by suggesting that he is speaking in his ministerial capacity. He can even refer a person to someone else for pastoral care.

This book on pastoral counselling is, therefore, not confined to the ordained person within some religious group, but it is intended for all those whose work brings them into close contact with other people, who are concerned about personal relationships, and who want to help those who find such relationships difficult. It is therefore written as much for the teacher and the nurse, for the social worker, the doctor and the lawyer, as it is for the priest and the minister. Hence it should be of help to the layman who is now being called upon to play an increasingly important part in matters which, in the past, had usually been restricted to those 'called to the ministry'.

On the other hand, this book makes no pretence at providing a deep psychological understanding of people's troubles, or what is sometimes described as Clinical Counselling. It is not intended to show how to help the deeply disturbed person. All that it does is to try to indicate some of the symptoms of disturbance and some of the ways in which more skilled help is available, so that the pastoral counsellor may know when he is unable to help a person himself and may be aware of other sources of assistance.

As indicated in the title, this book is merely an introduction. It tries to look at pastoral counselling in its social background, to discover its philosophical justification, and to suggest some of the principles to be followed and the methods which may be used. Hence various authorities are suggested in the bibliography at the end of the book, in connection both with the subject in general and with the subject matter of each chapter. It is hoped that this will lead the reader to a deeper study, and may also supply him with illustrations and with case histories which may help to make him more proficient in the practice of pastoral counselling.

I. Society and Counselling

Counselling, as a process of helping other people, has gained increasing popularity in recent years. It involves a relationship in which one person endeavours to help another to understand and to solve his difficulties of adjustment to society. From time immemorial individuals have talked over their personal concerns with acquaintances, friends and relatives, but counselling as such has only recently become a more formalised type of service with its own well-defined principles and methods of procedure. It is gradually superseding the giving of advice which for many years has been the more customary form of help and the one commonly used by the welfare worker, the doctor, the lawyer, the parson, the teacher and all those whose work brought them into contact with the personal needs of other people. Counselling can thus be seen as one of the modern ways of rendering personal service to others.

An important reason for this service is the growing sense of social responsibility and the conception that the well-being of an individual should be the concern of society as a whole. During the nineteenth century there gradually developed a far greater interest in the needs of other people less fortunate than oneself, and this led in the latter years to comprehensive programmes of social betterment which involved a new concept of society's duty to the individual. At first this was a concept of compassion and the giving of material help. Now, with the rising level of incomes, it has become the rendering of services of a personal nature which should help people to adjust themselves more easily to the many and varying demands of the complex society in which they live.

Another reason for the present development of counselling is the depth of understanding which the recent progress in psychology and sociology has made possible with regard to personal relationships and the reactions of different individuals to the problems which arise in their lives. At one time psychologists were mainly interested in the nature and identification of individual differences. Now they are far more concerned with people's behaviour and are attempting to explain such behaviour in terms of unconscious motivation and the effect that this has upon the reactions of the individual to the circumstances in which he finds himself. The justification for this sort of approach appears in the sociological surveys of small communities which have been conducted during the last few decades. They have revealed the many difficulties encountered by people in their endeavours to adjust themselves to the circumstances in which they are placed and the urgent need for personal counselling services of varying types to enable them to live happier and more satisfying lives.

Whatever form such counselling services take, the aim is always to help the person to feel more secure within himself so that he can cope more easily with the many difficulties or problems which may come his way. This involves the acquisition of a functional wholeness and a facility of adaptation to whatever circumstances may arise. Modern counselling has, therefore, been defined as 'assisting an individual to develop insight and ability to adjust to successive events in his life through the appraisal of his capacities, aptitudes and interests; helping him to understand motivations, emotional reactions and compensatory behaviour; and helping him attain a degree of personal integration whereby he can most effectively use his potentialities and make the greatest contribution to the society in which he lives'.[1]

The ancients were well aware of this need for integration, for in primitive society both the health of the body and of the soul were the care of the 'shaman' or medicine man, and for a

[1] References are given on p. 216.

long time these two aspects of the individual were interrelated. But this sense of integration did not persist. To the Greeks the care of the soul became the prerogative of the philosopher and was regarded as of far greater importance than the health of the body. Socrates himself claimed to be a healer of the soul, and it is from him that the word 'psychiatrist' is derived. This dichotomy continued in the early days of Christianity and the risk of losing one's soul was felt to be such a real and grave one for every human being that the health of the soul became a matter of mutual obligation and paternal care while that of the body was regarded with far less zest.

The same approach continued throughout the medieval period. Even the care of the soul became somewhat confused, for the aims and methods which were followed reflected the changing ideas with regard to the relative importance of the individual and the group. Where a high interpretation of group authority prevailed, the individual who broke the pattern of accepted behaviour was subjected to an authoritative corrective discipline. Thus there was a concern for the interest of the church rather than for the particular needs of the individual person and close attention was paid to specific acts, with a corresponding neglect of the more fundamental concept of the personal character as a whole, out of which the acts had sprung.

Luther tried to alter this by concentrating upon the development of the individual; and the German *Seelsorge*, or soul care, which was followed on the continent of Europe for several centuries, likened the pastor to a shepherd in charge of his sheep. But the Protestant Reformers did not entirely succeed in disentangling the individual from the group, for although the place of the spiritual adviser was taken by the theologian and the care of souls was largely carried on from the pulpit or in the process of home visiting, in some of the Protestant communions the individual received severe punishment if he did not follow the regulations of the church.

Nevertheless, the importance of the individual as a unified personality was not entirely forgotten and appears from time to time in the writings of different pastors. Richard Baxter, for instance, in *The Reformed Pastor* which was published in the mid-seventeenth century, thinks of his parishioners in these terms and by the eighteenth century certain German theologians were beginning to define the lines which the pastoral care of the individual should follow. This became more common in the nineteenth century, when a number of books appeared on what might be called practical theology, or the application of theological truths to everyday life. But these were more in the nature of hints and helps and contained little basic understanding of the person.

The developments in psychology and psychiatry of the early twentieth century were important factors leading to a change, since it became apparent that much of what a person did and felt was determined at a far deeper level than that of the conscious. It was gradually realised that unless all aspects of the personality received sufficient attention there was little chance that the person would feel secure as an individual. So, once again, the personality began to be regarded as a whole. At first this approach was put into practical use by the United States in the field of child guidance, and it has since developed into a widespread counselling movement which provides for almost every kind of problem or difficulty.

On the American continent, where counselling is spelt with only one 'l', it may imply a comparatively brief period of meetings between a person and a counsellor during which the counsellor, who has undergone an intensive technical and often clinical training, helps the person to sort out for himself some particular problem. Thus there is counselling in relation to marriage, to child care, in church, hospital and barracks, in prison, with the mentally sick and so on. In fact there is a great variety of forms of counselling related to particular types of problems.

American counselling can also go much deeper than this, and include some attempts to clarify motives so that it may shade into periods of psychotherapy when efforts are made to transform an unsatisfactory pattern of personality. On some occasions the actual counselling may not take place with the person himself, but with some other person closely related to him such as the mother of a child who needs help or with the wife of an alcoholic in the hope that a change in the environment in which a person lives will indirectly affect the person. Group counselling with more than one person at a time is quite common as, for example, talking matters over with the members of a family when there are family problems, or bringing together groups with similar problems when it is hoped that group interaction will help the individual members.

The application of these counselling methods to American pastoral counselling took place within a psychotherapeutic background. Anton T. Boisen, the chaplain at the Worcester State Hospital, Massachusetts, who had himself experienced a short but acute mental breakdown, started the plan in 1926 of bringing theological students into the hospital for three months of study and work. He was concerned that they should develop an understanding of the problems with which the patients were struggling, rather than that they should be interested in therapy, and that they should learn to recognise the spiritual dimensions of the problems which the patients faced. His work, in 1930, gave rise to the Council for Clinical Training and his methods very soon became part of the courses of many American seminaries which trained Protestant ministers. Thus his work and that of his colleagues have succeeded in integrating the principles of psychotherapy into the framework of the Christian ministry so that in America today there is a field of pastoral counselling which is distinct from other areas of psychotherapy and which is rapidly developing into a science of its own.

Leaders in this field are reluctant to identify themselves with any particular technique of counselling and often refuse even to label their own approach. Nevertheless, there is a tendency towards non-directive or what is sometimes called 'client-centred' counselling on the lines which Carl Rogers suggested in his book *Counseling and Psychotherapy*, published in 1942. Since then the emphasis has moved somewhat towards the relationship or communication between the counsellor and the person he is counselling. This has been elaborated by Carroll Wise in his book *Pastoral Counseling, Its Theory and Practise* (1951) and an account of the most recent methods used is given by Howard J. Clinebell in his book *Basic Types of Pastoral Counseling*.

In Britain, Dr Leslie Weatherhead was largely responsible for relating the new developments in psychology to pastoral care, and by the mid-'thirties he had established a clinic at the City Temple, London, of which he was the minister, for those needing psychiatric treatment as well as pastoral help. Other ministers and clergy, however, were slow to take up the challenge and it had to be kept alive by groups such as the Guild of Pastoral Psychology.

Similar experiments to those of Boisen were also made in Britain, although it was 1958 before any definite training in clinical theology was started. In that year Dr Frank Lake, who had been a medical missionary in Bengal and made an extensive study of the connections of psychology and theology, began to teach his methods to small groups of clergy. Such training had to be fitted in with the ordinary work of the parish priest and so it took the form of periodical seminars over a period of two years. Groups for the purpose were gradually formed in the different dioceses and increasing numbers of clergy attended. By 1962 a house at Nottingham had been purchased as a headquarters, and the Association for Clinical Theological Training and Pastoral Care was started as an educational charity. But pastoral counselling has not gone ahead at the same rate as in America, possibly because the link between theology and psychotherapy has not been satisfactorily resolved and many pastors still feel that important theological concepts are lost or watered down.

Nevertheless, the growing acceptance of the role and contribution of the behavioural sciences in our understanding of people's emotional difficulties is having an increasingly important meaning in the work of pastoral care. It is realised that it is necessary to know something of these developments if the pastor is to do his personal work successfully, and also if he is to know himself and the sort of reactions which he is likely to evoke in other people. Hence courses on these specific lines are being introduced into many of the theological colleges and colleges for the training of ministers, and into some of the syllabuses offered by the universities for the teaching of theology.

Many feel, however, that there is a danger that the pastoral counsellor will seek to become as proficient in mental healing as the psychiatrist. But a Danish writer puts it: 'Priest and physician have each their field of activity. These are of a different nature, and must not be blended. The priest may have to become expert in the knowledge of psychology and psychiatry not to exercise the art of mental healing, but for two reasons; partly to be able to recognise mental illness when they see it and to refer the sufferer from it to a physician, and partly to be able to impart a knowledge of the Gospel more effectively, especially to the mentally sick person who may have difficulty in understanding what Christianity is'.[2]

An important difference does exist between the work of the pastoral counsellor and that of the psychotherapist in that the pastoral counsellor is responsible for the help of any person who comes to him, whether ill or not, while the psychotherapist is concerned only with the sick who are usually recommended to him by a professional colleague. Therefore much of the work of the pastoral counsellor will be with those who happen to be passing through a time of temporary difficulty, or with people who are only slightly disturbed or emotionally upset.

Though he will follow principles and methods similar to those of psychotherapy, he will not do so at any depth, nor in a medically accepted manner. Should he feel it necessary to undertake psychotherapy himself, he needs medical recognition and to work under medical direction.

The pastoral counsellor, in the past, was regarded as the 'shepherd of souls', and sought to help those who came to him through what was then known as discipline, comfort and edification. One of the leading American authorities on modern pastoral counselling, Seward Hiltner, in his book *Preface to Pastoral Counseling* (1958), attempts to show how modern pastoral counselling retains this approach, but in a more up-to-date manner, using modern concepts with regard to personality and human relationships. Instead of discipline, comfort and edification healing, sustaining and guiding are substituted.

'Healing' replaces 'discipline' as more truly expressing the process of becoming well or 'whole'. 'Discipline' originally came from the same root as 'disciple' and meant schooling or training oneself for the task in hand. But it has long since changed its meaning. Instead healing takes over as a pastoral function which aims at overcoming some impairment in the personality, restoring the person to fitness and helping him to advance beyond his previous condition. The pastoral counsellor seeks to break through everything superficial and symptomatic to reach the casual and the basic need. He sees healing in its ultimate sense as a change in the direction of life, and he has the courage, sensitivity, persistence and restraint to make this his main purpose. Modern counselling is the contemporary way of achieving this and will usually help the less disturbed personality, although psychotherapy or counselling in depth is needed for the deeply disturbed.

Since the word 'comfort' has lost its original meaning of inspiring courage, upholding or standing with one who suffers, 'sustaining' has been substituted for it. When the nature of the problem is such that a person cannot be completely healed, then the sustaining aspect comes into operation. Sustaining means standing by, and relates to total situations which cannot be changed at all or which cannot be changed at the time, as, for example, with permanent bodily impairment or bereavement. Shock and loss are dominant in these situations, and at the crisis there is the need for silent companionship, followed later by consolation and enheartening. The counsellor does not give strength, but aids the sufferer to draw upon his own resources of strength that are potentially available to him. This is the purpose of supportive counselling, and although it may seem very like 'comfort' in its original sense, modern knowledge shows that the timing is often different. Negative feelings have to be dealt with, not merely brushed away as so often happened in the past, and doubt, instead of being criticised, has to be recognised as frequently a step to faith. Sustaining at its best produces a situation where a person is neither disgruntled that healing fails to eventuate nor discouraged because things cannot be changed.

'Edification' has given way to 'guiding', since this is the modern way of helping a person to keep to the path he has chosen. The counsellor as a guide is expected to know the land through which the person has to pass, to be familiar with the dangers peculiar to it and to have some idea of the goals that are relevant to the kind of search. But he is not in any sense a director in the way that implies coercion, for there are many things about which the guide knows less than the person he is guiding. On the other hand he cannot be coerced by the person, follow a method of which he disapproves, or seek a goal which he knows is illusory. He has to have the moral courage, when the timing is right, to introduce the standards and values in which he believes. He edifies in the sense that he benefits the person spiritually, but he is very careful how and when he does so. Guiding cannot be legalistic or authoritative, for unless guiding helps a person to make contact with something felt as his own it will not finally be effective.

A great deal of guiding is, in fact, educative counselling and so can fall under the theological concept of sanctification, since healing, salvation or redemption have in some significant sense taken place, with a resultant need for information and instruction. Similarly, after an acute crisis, spiritual help is often needed to bring the threads together to form a new pattern of life. But guiding may have no apparent spiritual content and be just a helping hand to enable a person to be himself again and to play his part in the community.

Healing, sustaining and guiding are not confined to the person-to-person relationship of pastoral counselling, but they need as well a group within which the person can become a part and which will receive him as one of themselves. This implies a therapeutic community which is ready to accept those who have been finding life difficult and who, as the result of successful counselling, are trying to establish themselves in society. The counsellor who is also a minister of religion usually has his church and this is the fellowship on which he should be able to rely to help those who come to him for health, sustaining and guiding. Other counsellors may also be members of a church which welcomes such people, or they may be linked with a group which exists to help those who, for the moment, find it difficult to stand on their own feet.

The counsellor cannot usually help a person unless he also takes into account the background from which the person comes. This background is partly the outcome of the customs and culture of the community as a whole, and partly depends upon the various social groups to which the person belongs. Every community has its objects, ideals, knowledge, habits, values and attitudes and there are usually customary and standardised ways of doing things which are common to those sharing a particular culture. A person learns these from the previous generation and in this way is expected to be able to cope with his own environment and with his relationships with other people. These things will also vary according to the position or role which a person holds in his family, in his work group, among the people with whom he spends his leisure time, and in the community at large, and he needs to know what is expected of him in each particular role that he holds.

Hence there develop certain patterns of behaviour to which a person is expected to conform. These behaviour patterns will be fairly flexible, but there will be limits beyond which a person cannot go, and anyone who exceeds these limits will soon find that he is ostracised by many of his fellows, and may even come within the ambit of the law.

The counsellor has to be aware of the demands that society can make upon a person and to what extent the person is able and willing to meet these demands. Very few people desire to forge a path entirely on their own, or are in a position to challenge the demands which society makes upon them. Most have to fit into the pattern which society offers and their trouble usually lies in the fact that for one reason or another they are unable to do so. Inability to fit into the prevailing pattern of society usually occurs because a person does not know or understand its standards or values, because he is incapable for some reason of following them, or because he can only make immature decisions. Counselling should help him in these respects and so make it possible for him to adapt himself more easily to the society in which he lives, and to feel more comfortable and happy. It does not take away his freedom of choice, but it helps him to exercise this choice with a greater degree of maturity and wider knowledge about the relevant circumstances.

In a relatively static society people find it easier to conform to the acknowledged patterns of behaviour, since they have learnt them from their childhood, and know what to expect when difficulties arise. When change occurred in the past it was at a far more leisurely rate, and the individual was usually able to adjust himself to it. Now the world seems to be changing more rapidly than the human power of adjustment and, even if it were so desired, no power at present is able to control this rate of change.

The speed of change has made it far more difficult for people to understand one another. We no longer live in small, cohesive communities, knowing our neighbours well, and being familiar with the general tenor of their lives. Instead we are constantly on the move, so much so that the average family in Britain changes house once in seven years, and the average American even more frequently. Thus friendships tend to be superficial and we rarely reach the deeper levels of understanding one another that come from being together for a reasonably long time. Things which in the past could have been discussed with an intimate friend now are not mentioned at all and may never come to the surface, except in the counsellor's study.

Communication is also made more difficult by the extent of specialisation which is reached in the different aspects of life. Terms are used by one group which are quite incomprehensible to another, and are sometimes misunderstood. Methods of approach vary, and those who are trained in one method may find extreme difficulty in following the paths of those trained in another. For instance, people familiar with the traditional methods of education may find the therapeutic training group, where the members spend their time studying the group and the processes of social interaction that take place in it, not only trying but emotionally upsetting.

These difficulties in communication lead to a widening gap between the generations. Half a century ago parents could assume that their children would grow up in a world recognisably like their own. Now the older generation has little comprehension or understanding of the world in which young people live, and they themselves often find it difficult to adjust to their own world. This has its effect not only upon family relationships, but upon all groups where the generations meet. The counsellor is inevitably called upon to interpret the outlook of one generation to another.

These are perhaps the more superficial facets of change. Underlying these, and of a more traumatic effect, are the changes which are taking place in the traditional ethical and moral values. Such values, which have been accepted almost without question for many generations, are now being criticised and thrown aside. To take a minor example, the coming of the welfare state has produced an entirely new perspective with regard to making provision for one's children and for the old. Whereas a generation or so ago members of a family felt a keen responsibility for one another, now most people would regard much of this responsibility as belonging to the state. This is happening in many other spheres of life as well, so that as the patterns and techniques of social life change, moral problems alter their form, and the conventional answers to the conventional questions no longer fit reality.

Those who have the courage to seek a new approach often do so under great adverse pressure, and this may leave its mark both upon their own personalities and also upon those of their critics. At the opposite end of the scale are those who in this age of moral confusion and shifting values decide to have no standards at all. Most people lie somewhere between these two extremes and have the sneaking feeling that they should be more definite in their views and yet fear to be so. This tends to breed a state of anxious confusion often expressed outwardly by a show of bravado.

Fundamentally this confusion arises from the conflict between the unprecedented security at the conscious level of people's lives and the insecurity deep down. Most material needs are now met and the fear of grinding poverty, painful illness and a lack of medical care have lost much of their sting. Yet, within, people are often in a great state of fear and perturbation. A firm faith and a belief in something beyond themselves is no longer so sure.

They feel adrift and in a world where the individual has less and less value. It is hardly surprising that there is a great deal of disillusionment and cynicism and a shrugging off of authority. Not only is this apparent among the young in our schools and universities, but it is one of the difficulties which faces the modern pastor, who no longer is regarded in the position of authority which he used to hold, and yet is still felt by many people to be different from themselves and so not easily approachable or only approachable in a superficial manner. This is one of the greatest difficulties which the clergy have to meet if they are to be successful pastoral counsellors.

The modern pastor is convinced that the Christian faith has resources that can enable a person to become what he feels he should be, but in the climate of modern society it is extremely difficult to convey this to people. The man in the street usually has very little use for Christianity, and even less for the church. This is partly because he has never fully understood the real meaning of Christianity and judges the value of the faith by the behaviour of some of the Christians he has met. It is also partly due to the fact that the church has failed to keep up with the changes in society. In the nineteenth century the church entered into a controversy with science which it still has to live down. It made the mistake of assuming that the supernatural could be identified with the unnatural, and that the finger of God could be detected in those events for which no natural explanation was forthcoming. The further science extended her frontiers, the less room this left for God. Today the church realises that she has no quarrel with science as such, and the more thoughtful scientists know that science does not exclude religion. But few other people are convinced of this.

The church has also tended to concentrate upon private morality and to pay far less attention to social morality. It has had a great deal to say about individual behaviour, and very little to comment upon the behaviour of the group or of the community as a whole. Such things as industrial and race relations which are favourite topics today have been given comparatively little attention either by the church at large or by individual church communities. This has made the non-church-goer feel that Christianity has little to say about his everyday life with his fellow men. On the other hand the church-goer often tends to place religion in a small compartment of his life which is quite cut off from the things of every day.

Therefore the minister of religion starts at a disadvantage with the ordinary counsellor. Not only does he have all the usual difficulties of the counselling process, but he has to be alert all the time to the possibility of introducing the person to the inner meaning of Christianity. And he has to do so in spite of the imperfect interpretation of the church, and in spite of its inadequate embodiment and expression in the lives of Christian people and Christian communities.

He has a further difficulty, in that people do not readily come to him. For many centuries of the Christian era pastoral counselling has been almost entirely in the hands of those ordained to the Christian ministry and people have looked up to such counsellors and been ready to take their troubles to them. The present decline in religious practices has not only reduced the number of ordained ministers, but the outlook of the people towards them is changed. They are no longer regarded as people who possess a fund of knowledge and wisdom which is not generally available. In fact they are often thought to be out of date and out of touch with the ordinary everyday world and its problems. Far fewer church members and even fewer non-church people than in the past feel like going to their clergyman or minister when in difficulty. Instead they seek advice and help from other members of the community.

The doctor is frequently the person to whom they turn, for as the sociologist, Talcott Parsons, points out, he has 'very important associations with the realm of the sacred'.[3] His intimate contact with people, his familiarity with the crises of life and death, and his position in society as a person of reliability and integrity give him a certain professional charisma which has marked him out and made him a successor to the pastor of earlier times. This is not necessarily confined to modern times, for there have always been doctors who have played the parts of confidential personal adviser and of moral counsellor. But today, when people are looking for someone in whom to confide and who will give them sound advice, particularly at times of pain and impending death, they will turn to those who are in the closest contact with them, and this is frequently the doctor.

With the development of psychological medicine and the recognition that many an illness of the body is very closely related to a sickness of the mind there has been a growth in the practice of psychoanalysis and of psychiatry so that those who might previously have gone to the person or even to the doctor now seek help in one or other of these new ways. It is largely the small numbers of psychoanalysts and psychiatrists in this country and the high fees that are charged for private patients which set a limit to those who are able to consult them.

The family lawyer and the school teacher also share in this work of counselling. Many who for one reason or another prefer not to divulge details of their personal life to anyone else feel more at ease with a lawyer who probably has no social contact with them. The teacher is frequently the friend and adviser of his pupils, and even of their parents when he makes a point of getting to know them.

But by far the largest group of modern counsellors are the numbers of social workers who are to be found in many different and specialised forms of social work and who come into contact with a wide diversity of people in the course of their daily tasks. The majority of these workers already have some knowledge of counselling through their training in social casework, and they use these methods in their numerous contacts with the people among whom they work. Thus there is quite a body of people who, as part of their daily work, are engaged in counselling of a pastoral nature.

The need for such counsellors is likely to increase in the future, for our affluent society, with its technological advances and large scale organisations, makes relationships more and more impersonal. Yet if people are to be happy and contented they must understand one another better and be able to fit more easily into the groups to which they belong. This is true not only in industrial and social life, but wherever people come together in large numbers. There is a growing recognition of the importance of good personal relationships in every sphere of life and we are at last beginning, in this country, to realise that counselling services are needed by people of all ages and descriptions and to expect them to be available wherever the size of the group makes interpersonal relationships difficult.

These counselling services do not differ greatly from those which have always been known as pastoral counselling. Paul Halmos, in his stimulating book, *The Faith of the Counsellors*, has shown how closely the basic principles of these counsellors correspond with the ideas of Christianity. He attributes to them a belief, which they themselves would rarely confess, that counselling has justification of a moral and metaphysical nature, and that these elements permeate the technical procedures and become themselves an essential part of the counselling process. They have come to realise that their personal intervention is much more effective when it is carried out with spontaneous warmth and affection, or what might be called Christian love, than when motives of interest and concern are all that are expressed. They take the fundamental ambivalences of life, the alternating impulsives of loving and hating, as basic to their work, and yet they are firm believers at the same time in the supreme rationality and intelligence of life. They regard the individual whom they are helping as a person and respect his personal integrity, and do not seek to impose their own preferences upon him. They use the scientific techniques which they have learnt and yet their counselling is not a purely mechanical affair, but is a real act of caring and helping.

Counselling of any type has to have a very large element of faith, for like the doctor, the counsellor is only an intermediary in the process of healing. He can use all his scientific knowledge and skill, but more than this is needed to restore the person to health. There has to be an underlying assumption that health can be restored, and the person has to be supported until this takes place. There is no proof that this will happen, but both the counsellor and the person being counselled believe that it will. Thus there is a very close similarity between the forms of counselling carried on by these varied groups of people today, and what for a very long time has been known as pastoral counselling. The main difference lies in the fact that such counsellors will not necessarily introduce into their counselling any reference to their religious beliefs or be in a position to offer the spiritual resources of some religious denomination.

Hence a distinction is often made between pastoral counselling and pastoral care. Pastoral counselling is regarded as the process of caring for the human being as a person in all the aspects of his nature and endeavouring to help him to become a whole and mature person. It follows very similar methods to ordinary counselling and takes heed of all the advances that are made in this field. It is carried on not only by ministers of religion but by educationalists, social workers, doctors and lawyers and many others who come in close contact with people's personal needs either as part of their everyday work or as members of some local counselling centre.

Pastoral care, on the other hand, is concerned with the giving of spiritual help, as in the case of the priest or pastor when he makes available the spiritual resources of the church to which the person belongs. This would include the benefits of the sacraments and the help which can be derived from the reading of the scriptures or from prayer.

This distinction is often extremely difficult to make, and may in some cases be quite impossible but most modern pastors, in their counselling, do try to make it and only offer pastoral care when it is asked for by the person concerned or when the person happens to be a member of their own particular church. This is the attitude adopted by most of the counselling centres in this country. Although they usually claim some initial connection with the churches they do not advertise this fact so that it is possible for anyone in need of help to seek their services. In practice they find that only a very small proportion of those who come to them have any special religious affiliation. It is also the attitude of the many other people who, in the course of their daily work and personal contacts, find themselves in the role of a pastoral counsellor.

It is for all these people that this book has relevance. It will therefore first be concerned with counselling in general, and with its affinities to some of the other disciplines to which it is closely linked. It will then connect these basic ideas to what has been commonly called pastoral counselling. This method of approach has two justifications. The basic principles of counselling should be fundamental to whatever form this counselling may take; and pastoral counselling, in the sense in which it has been defined, needs to be understood not only by the clergyman and minister but by all who are engaged in any of the helping services or who are in close personal relationships with other people.

II. Persons in Relationship

Throughout the ages man has asked the question: Who am I? and has found a great variety of answers, and the very fact that he is able to ask this question, to stand aside from himself and look at himself, and reach some conclusive decision about himself, distinguishes him from the other orders of creation. He is a learning, conceptual being, able to take account of the circumstances in which he lives, to improve upon them and come to some sort of conclusion about them. He is also able to look beyond himself, to catch some glimpses of a world outside himself and to conceive of a Being greater than himself.

A knowledge of the nature of man can be sought along two routes. One proceeds by logical analysis and precise assessment. It is objective and scientific, and follows the course of intellectual information. It takes account of how he appears to others and the motives which actuate his behaviour. The other is subjective and intuitive and involves a total understanding and a spiritual communion. It is concerned with the man 'himself'—that elusive, incoherent, complicated and ambiguous being that is known as a 'person'. Neither route on its own will ever reach the 'real' or complete person, but if both routes are followed together there is a greater likelihood of coming somewhere nearer to it.

It is the façade of a person, or what is sometimes called the mask or 'persona' which we discover when we set out along the first route to find what man is like. This provides the image of the person in the context of the scenery of his life, the history of his people, the background of his family, his job, his social contacts and his culture. And even this may not be completely true to fact, for it is influenced by the outlook, background and whole environment of the observer as well. It is possible to take account of these different facts and so to learn something about the person, but this does not necessarily mean that we know very much about the 'real' person. It is only by following the second route and by seeking desperately hard to understand an individual and trying 'to be' this individual for a moment that it is possible to get a glimpse of the 'real' person, and this is usually only fleeting and rarely very precise. To distinguish the person from the 'persona' is a continuous and endless task. But as the observer increases in his understanding of the individual, the way becomes prepared for a personal encounter, and a personal encounter opens the road for a more penetrating and objective observation. Thus the discerning observer may begin to pierce through the façade which is the start to an understanding of the 'real' or complete person.

Man can be regarded from different aspects or dimensions and these correspond very roughly to what are sometimes called the body, mind and spirit. In actual fact, these aspects are entirely artificial and by no means isolated from one another, since there is no living body without mind, nor mind without body. But if a complex being like man is to be studied, it is necessary to make some sort of artificial, intellectual distinction.

For this purpose the body can be regarded as the material presentation of the person in space and time. It is how the person appears on first sight. Because the body is conceived at a definite moment in time and thereafter is organised and developed according to natural laws governing its form, it is also subject to the inevitable limitations of time and eventually it dies. Man shares with all other living things, plants or animals, this coming into being, living and passing away.

The psychical aspect of man is concerned with what goes on in his mind. For many centuries it was thought that conscious control could be exercised over this, and that although there was an unconscious part, it was only very small and insignificant.

Recent psychologists, Jung in particular, have shown that this is by no means so; in fact quite the reverse. A great part of man's psychical aspect consists of the unconscious and only a very small part of this is within the range of recall. Much lies buried deep down, and can only be brought to the surface by some external process such as psychoanalysis. Furthermore the Jungian school holds that a part consists of strange, primitive forms or archetypes which are the remnants of an earlier culture and mode of expression.

The aspect of the person which is to a special degree directed towards God may be regarded as man's spiritual aspect. Man has always looked outside himself to some greater power or beings and because he cannot perceive what such beings are really like has dressed them in various forms, sometimes projecting their qualities on to actual individuals, and then treating them as if they really existed. This is the vast domain of religion which is a strange world, pregnant with power, and which man usually feels he can only approach with the appropriate ritual and ceremonies.

The importance accorded to these different ways of looking at a person is highly variable. Many rate the spiritual aspect extremely low and a few refuse to recognise it. Some think that the body controls the mind and others that the mind controls the body. Medical science has for a long time segregated the physical aspect and sought to deal with it purely by mechanistic means. But just as it is becoming accepted that diseases show themselves as both physical and psychical disturbances at the same time, and that these are more or less reversible, so there is a growing realisation that it is neither the body that controls the mind, nor the mind the body, but rather that they are at one and the same time the indivisible reality of that illusive thing that we call the person. There are those who are of the opinion that it is an inner spiritual force, man's spiritual destiny, which controls both his body and his mental phenomena, whether normal or pathological. Thus the body and mind may be only the means of the expression of the spirit which co-ordinates and directs them both at once.

This is the framework which the pastoral counsellor accepts as the basis for his counselling. It is complicated by the fact that no simple scientific discipline can help him in his search for the 'real' or complete person. The physical sciences can observe and treat the body or the physical aspect of a person. Psychology can attempt to understand and interpret his mind or what is sometimes called his 'soul'. Philosophy can give some account of his spiritual aspect. But full comprehension of man as an indivisible totality will always elude the grasp of the counsellor and this is why he will only manage to gain glimpses of the 'real' person.

A distinguishing feature of man is his personal self-consciousness, that is the consciousness which he has of a 'not-self', or of an external world from which he can distinguish himself, which he can observe objectively from without and with which he can enter into relationship, or not, as he feels inclined.

Psychologists have described the growth of self-consciousness as a double movement, first of separation from others and then of relation between the self and things. It is as a child becomes aware of his own 'individuality' that he begins to be a person. He then begins to realise that he is distinct from other people and can, if he so desires, enter into personal relationships with them. Self-consciousness implies both an awareness of oneself by oneself, and an awareness of oneself as an object of someone else's observation. These two forms of awareness are necessary for an individual to develop his personality and to come nearer to being a 'real' person.

We become aware of ourselves by ourselves both as part of a world of matter and of organic life. On the material level we have an objective consciousness of material things. This knowledge is not only a knowledge of ourselves as material objects, but it is also a knowledge of our dependence upon the existence of material objects. We live as members of the material world, and since we are conscious of this we already know ourselves as something more than material.

Similarly at the level of organic life we know ourselves as living beings. We are conscious of living as members of a society of organic beings and in dependence upon such a society. We live as organisms in a world of life and our consciousness that we are individual organisms is a consciousness that we belong as dependent individuals to a world of organic reality. We are able to assert our animal nature because we already have a consciousness of ourselves as something over and above animal life.

It is as part of a world of personality that we become aware of ourselves as objects of someone else's observation. It is in and through our consciousness of other persons that we really begin to know ourselves as persons, and as we begin to know ourselves in this way so we begin to become 'real' persons. There can be no such thing as a 'real' person who is isolated. It is only in relationship between oneself and another person that the self can live. The very essence of self is that there is a difference between I and You. There is no I without You. The relationship between persons constitutes their individualities.

Relationships can be of two types, either personal or impersonal, according to whether a person's attitude to another individual is that of person-to-person, or of person-to-thing. As Martin Buber points out in his treatise *I and You* (published in German in 1923) there is a radical difference between a man's attitude to other men and his attitude to things. The attitude to other men is a relation between persons; to things it is a connection with objects. In the person-to-person relationship one subject, I, confronts another subject, Thou. In an impersonal relationship the subject, I, contemplates and experiences an object, It. These two attitudes represent the basic twofold situations of human life, the former constituting the world of Thou, and the latter the world of It.

A man can approach another person as a Thou, that is in a way that treats him as a person, or he can approach him as an It, which means regarding the other person as an object. In an I-Thou relationship the other person is not just a he or a she but a reality. The Thou meets me and I step into direct relation with this person. The characteristic situation is one of meeting, and in this situation there is no reduction of the I or Thou. So long as I remain in relationship with my Thou I cannot know him as someone from outside but can only know him in the relationship itself. The relationship is mutual and personal. On the other hand, in the I-It relationship, or what is called an impersonal relationship, the other is not regarded as a person, but as a man or an object, possessing certain capacities and characteristics which make him useful.

The world in which we live is a world of activity, set in the context of space and time. Very soon an I-Thou relationship becomes worked out or permeated with a means, so that the Thou becomes an object among objects, though it may still remain the most important of these objects. Nevertheless, the Thou has become an It and the relationship impersonal. Every Thou in the world is fated by the nature of things to become an It, or a means to an end; for without It man cannot live. Thus the impersonal aspect in every relationship is always there though it may be subordinated to a personal aspect for a time. Most direct relationships follow a process of withdrawal and return from the personal to the impersonal, though these processes are usually confusedly entangled and rarely take place in clear succession. It is only indirect relationships which remain permanently impersonal. Direct relationships must sometimes take the I-Thou form, for unless they do the parties to the relationship are hardly human.

There is only one Thou that never becomes an It, the Eternal Thou, and that is God. Though we may speak of God in the third person, the reality of his approach is constituted in the fullness of the relation of an I with a Thou, thus vindicating the fact that He concerns himself not only with the destiny of the world as a whole, but with that of every person within the world. As John Oman points out: 'this offers the assurance of a gracious relation to us which would at once cease were it impersonal in its dealing or restricted in the sphere of its goodness. Its whole quality and distinction is to seek to be personal on both sides, and if any aspect of life had to be exempted from its wise and loving dealing, we should never know where next it might fail'.[4]

People may enter into relationship with one another for two very different purposes. In the first place they associate with each other in order to achieve some purpose which they all share. Out of this there springs a life of social co-operation through which they provide for their common needs and achieve their common ends. The characteristic of this form of social life is its purpose. There is always some special purpose for getting together for associating and co-operating in this particular way. But because of this the persons involved cannot enter into this form of relationship with the whole of themselves. The purpose for which they get together is always only one of their many purposes, for there are other purposes which cannot be achieved by this association.

For example, a professional society brings people together for a purpose which goes to the very roots of social life, and can even at times command loyalties which its members might be prepared to defend against other forms of social organisation. But it is not a personal association, since its basis is a common purpose, and since its members enter it in virtue of one particular aspect of their humanity. They are not members because they are human beings, but because they have a special professional interest in common with all the others. This gives an exclusive character to the association because only individuals who share that particular interest are qualified for membership. It also, for the same reason, restricts the range of human interest the association serves, for all its members have other interests which cannot be served by the professional association. This is the reason why men cannot enter into such associations as persons, with the whole of themselves.

All organised relationships are of this kind, even if the organisation is not enforced by law or rule of membership, but only by custom or public opinion. Wherever an organisation is found, it is a group which exists for a purpose and which therefore cannot include people as persons but only as people who are interested in that particular purpose or function of the group. The whole complex of the activities of human life is generalised in this way, and this is what is usually meant by society, or by the social life.

The second reason for which people enter into relationships with one another is purely in order to express their whole selves to one another in mutuality and friendship. The relationship between them has no purpose beyond itself. They associate because it is natural for human beings to share their experiences, to understand one another, to find joy and satisfaction in being together and in expressing and revealing themselves to one another. It is this field of human relationships which constitutes what is called the personal life, and it is the only way in which people can live as persons at all and the only form of human life in which they can be their whole selves. There is no ulterior motive behind their coming together. It is not based on particular interests, nor does it serve partial or limited ends. The value of the relationship lies entirely in the persons concerned and it transcends all other values. This is perhaps best illustrated in a happy marriage.

As John Macmurray puts it, the personal life 'is the life which we live as persons, and we can live it only by entering into relationships with other people on a fully personal basis, in which we give ourselves to one another; or, to put the same thing the other way round, in which we accept one another freely for what we are, and in which therefore there is and can be no purpose other than the sharing of our lives in fellowship. The impulse to do this is simply the impulse to be ourselves completely;

and not to gain anything, nor to achieve anything, but simply to be ourselves as fully and completely as it is possible. . . . The social life and the individual life can only be subordinate to this. They are necessary as a basis for this. In other words, the whole network of organised human association has only one meaning; that it is the necessary foundation on which the personal life can be built,'[5]

There are two fundamental distinctions between social and personal life. One involves the equality of persons. In all functional associations the place of the individual is determined by the particular service which he renders to the general purpose of the whole, and these functional relationships largely depend upon differences of skill and capacity for different tasks. The proper organisation of society depends upon suiting people to their functions and the way that this is done is to use the natural differences between people to fit them for different tasks and services to the community. It is obvious and necessary from this point of view that people should not be equal. But in the personal life there is no reason why relationships should be based upon these natural functional differences. Personal relationships are relationships between individuals as persons and their functional differences have nothing directly to do with the relationship, though they may have a great deal to do with its quality and character and the ways in which it expresses itself. Personal relationships are possible between any two persons just because they are persons, though they may be difficult in some cases, and meagre in others. Once a personal relationship is established the differences between the persons concerned are the stuff out of which the texture of their fellowship is woven, and provided the equal relationship is maintained, it is precisely the differences that enrich the relationship.

The second distinction between the social and the personal life is that the personal life is the life of freedom. The institutional life of society exists only through the imposition of restraints, even if they are self-imposed, for only in this way is it possible to get people to conform. But the personal life is that life in which people are seeking freedom in their relations with one another. They are trying to accept one another and to be accepted for what they are, so that they can be themselves and express themselves to one another. It is only in such a way that it is possible to live spontaneously in a free and full expression as persons without constraint.

Personal life is, therefore, essentially a life of relations between people, and it differs from the social life in that it is entered into with the whole of ourselves. It demands a relationship in which we can be our whole selves and have complete freedom to express everything that makes us feel what we are. The need is for a fully positive relation in which we trust one another and so can think, feel and act together. If we quarrel, as we are bound to do from time to time, the relationship is temporarily broken. Each withdraws from the other into himself, and the trust is replaced by fear. We can no longer be ourselves in relation to one another. Since we are in conflict each loses his freedom and must act under constraint. We may agree to co-operate on conditions which impose a restraint upon each of us, and which prevent the outbreak of active hostility. In this case we remain isolated individuals, and the co-operation between us, though it may appear to satisfy our need of one another, will not really satisfy us. On the other hand, there can be a reconciliation which restores the original confidence so that the negative motivation is overcome and the positive relation re-established.

Where there is complete confidence in relationships a fellowship, or what is sometimes called a 'community' is formed. Its members are united in a positive and common motivation. They act together and in unison. The group is constituted and maintained by mutual affection, and this can be so only when each member of the group is in a positive personal relation to each of the others taken separately. The structure of such a group or 'community' is the nexus or network of the active relations of friendship between all possible pairs of its members.

Community or fellowship is found in any group where there is not merely a common life, but also a consciousness of the common life. This is particularly true of the social institution known as the family, which is the basis as well as the origin of all subsequent communities. The family pattern is the norm to which other communities tend to correspond. It is neither established by force nor maintained by a sense of duty, but it is established and maintained by natural affection, which is a conscious and positive motive in its members. The members should care for one another sufficiently to have no need to fear one another. The normal positive motivation is usually sufficient to dominate the negative motives of self-interest and individualism. Thus the more a group approximates to this family pattern, the more it realises itself as a community.

Such community or fellowship can also be found in the church, the club, the factory, the office or any place where people are together. Its basic problem is that of overcoming fear and subordinating the negative motivation to the positive in the personal relationships of one with another. This is the basic problem of all personal life. All others are contained in the problem of maintaining the network of positive personal relationships which constitute a human community. Such a community is not an organisation but is the living of a personal life in common, so that any human group becomes a community in so far as its normal outlook is communal and involves a positive approach to one another.

The aim of the counsellor is to make possible this sort of personal life and personal relationship, and this can only be achieved when the persons themselves are capable of forming such relations with other people. It is the mature, whole or integrated person who is in this position and so it becomes the counsellor's purpose to help people to become whole. To be whole means to be reconciled to those sides of the personality which may have been overlooked or not even recognised. Such a person must have reached a balance between the different aspects of his personality, both of those of which he is conscious and of those of which he is not fully conscious. This is the process which the psychologists often call individuation.

The socially mature personality is one who has been allowed to develop his natural tendencies harmoniously in an atmosphere of security. His inner control over his emotions is effortless and he has them at his full disposal for the task of real life. He has a clear and spontaneous capacity to assert his own values without fear and anxious consideration and he is not troubled by inner tensions resulting from secret needs for such things as power and vengeance. This frees his natural aggressiveness from the venom of hostility, self-contradiction and feelings of guilt. It imparts a quality of peaceful strength and purposefulness to his character, and the strength is balanced by an equally mature capacity for love and tenderness in his relations with other human beings. There is no cheap and easy way to an integrated personality but it involves an honest facing of ourselves with the moral courage to refuse to evade our own problems by projecting them on to other people.

It is necessary to learn to make sound ethical judgements, and to have one's feelings and impulses back these judgements rather than to oppose them. This means developing a conscious understanding and knowledge of moral and spiritual values, and an emotional life which likes and desires what we pronounce as 'good'. Very early in our personal experience we notice what interests us and attend to it, and the rest of what there is is overlooked. In fact, we make a value judgement, and this is inherent in every choice. At first little more than an automatic and blind acceptance of externally imposed standards is possible, but gradually the capacity to reflect on the distinctions which others make between good and bad is developed. We gradually learn not only to accept but to question, and to question not merely rebelliously but in a fair-minded and objective way. As our private individual conscience casts off much that is social code and custom of previous generations, it grows towards perception of that objective system of values which the universal experience of mankind finds to be good in living in personal relationships.

Most adults have a conscience which is a curious mixture of customary attitudes and independent judgements and they usually manage satisfactorily, unless some deep experience shakes them up. But many people do not mature to this extent, and even in adulthood still adopt an attitude of blind submissiveness or hostile rejection of authority. This will usually prevent integration and will fill the personality with tension and anxiety. These are the sorts of people whom the counsellor will be meeting constantly. His task will be to help them to achieve the state of mind where they can make sincere and true value judgements for themselves.

Troubles may also be related to character. In other words it is not only the ethical quality of a person, but his basic emotional organisation, the conscious and still more the unconscious motives, desires, feelings, attitudes and conflicts that affect his reactions to events and people. It is not so much what happens to a person, as what he feels and does about it, that matters, and this is by no means always governed by his own choice. Most of us are suffering from some degree of conflict which reveals itself perhaps in the mildest way, in lapses of speech or of memory, in misunderstanding of what we have heard or read, or in other people's motives. At the other extreme lie the traumatic cases of lost memory, hysterical paralysis, blindness and deafness. In between these two extremes are numerous anxieties, fears and obsessions from which the sufferer is quite unable to free himself, and by which he is often drawing attention to the need for help. It is here that the need for another person arises, who will be qualified to understand his difficulties, and so be able to help him to overcome them and to meet the demands of life with courage and with comparative success.

The counsellor, who is also a pastor, cannot be content with offering his help in human relationships alone. He is as much concerned with a person's relationship with God, and with a God who cares personally for people, who concerns Himself with individuals, and who is aware of all that is happening to them. This God does not only love all men in general, but each in particular. He concerns himself not only with human destiny as a whole, but with the destiny of every person.

People, who have been touched by this relationship, realise their full potential. Their stature increases and bursts the bounds of their existing form. For man is not a fixed datum, but a potential person, a plan known to God with a life which God can direct day by day towards its fulfilment. However carefully and candidly a man examines himself, he can, by himself, rarely find what God is capable of awakening in him. The pastoral counsellor is frequently surprised by the extent to which this happens. It is the possibilities of this divine relationship which gives him encouragement when human relationships seem to have failed and when there seems little more that he can do to help the person.

Through these two I-Thou relationships with God and with one's fellow men it is possible to cast off the façades of the personality and to begin to become a 'real' or complete person, thus changing the whole nature of our being. All other relationships take on a new character in the light of these relationships. They become shot through with a glow which was absent when they were merely the fulfilment of a function. Everything becomes the occasion for a personal contact and for a chance to understand others, the personal factors which underlie their behaviour, their relations and their opinions. It becomes much more interesting, as well as more important to understand why someone has a certain failing, than to be irritated by it; to understand why he maintains a certain point of view than to combat it; to listen to confidences than to judge appearances. The atmosphere of the home, the office, or the factory is rapidly transformed when personal fellowship is established between those who previously criticised or ignored one another. It is in this way that the 'persona' gives way to the person. We no longer continue to be cold, objective, impersonal observers, watching the operation of blind and inexorable mechanisms, but persons, with other persons around us, seeking to establish a personal bond with them.

Unfortunately nobody manages entirely to cast off the façade that he has acquired and to become that self which he truly is. But he may desire to do so, and may want to get away from his superficial appearance, from the things he feels he ought to do, from meeting expectations and from pleasing others, to being what he inwardly and actually is. The purpose of pastoral counselling is to help him to do this. It encourages him to listen to the deepest recesses of his physiological and emotional being and so helps him to become more truly himself both in his relationships with other people and with God. For some people it is just a matter of a helping hand in the problems of daily living and an encouragement when these become increasingly burdensome. For others it may require a deeper and more penetrating perception of the reasons for an inability to make satisfactory relationships. But in every case it involves a step towards maturity and a shaking off of a part of the 'persona' to reveal something more of the 'real' person.

III. A New Understanding of People

Throughout the centuries individuals have, in a variety of ways, used face-to-face situations in an endeavour to help people with their problems and anxieties. Parents have warned and advised their children; pledges and promises have been made; auto-suggestion has been used; and people have been encouraged to refer their problems and difficulties to some father confessor whose greater knowledge was expected to produce some solution. No doubt a great deal of help was received, and many people were enabled to face life with a greater confidence. But the giving of such help was very much a matter of luck. Some people had the gift for it and others learnt by experience. Few understood exactly what they were doing, and were very rarely aware of any side effects which might result from their advice and admonition.

The study of human behaviour and experience has made great strides in recent decades. A great deal more is now known about the human personality than was the case in the past. Until the 1920's psychology was not usually regarded as a science of human behaviour, but formed part of moral philosophy and was concerned either with medical science in the form of neurology, or with the human instincts or emotions, as one finds in William McDougall's *Social Psychology* which first was published in 1908. Now psychology, with its helpmate psychiatry, seeks to explain human behaviour at all levels of human experience.

We can think of the human being as equipped with the capacity to make responses both to the stimuli of the outside world and to those arising within himself. In their most simple form the responses to stimuli appear to be entirely automatic and based upon the mechanism which is called reflex action, and this presents essentially an unvarying pattern of stimulus and response. That part of human behaviour which is served entirely by reflexes is concerned chiefly with such things as balance, the blinking of the eye, and the regulation of internal processes such as digestion and breathing.

More complicated patterns of behaviour which depend to a small but to a certain extent on conscious deliberation and control are our instincts. Human beings are born with a number of powerful instincts which develop during childhood and adolescence. The more important of these are the instincts of self-preservation, of sex, and what is known as the herd or communal instinct. An individual instinctively wards off an attack of some kind; he is attracted often unwittingly by a member of the opposite sex, and when in danger he seeks security in the company of others.

The way in which an individual becomes aware of an instinct is by the urge or tension of the feeling experience, and this will invariably be accompanied by certain bodily changes. For example, fear may be shown by pallor, grief by tears, and anger by flushing. The pattern of expression of these instincts and the emotions which accompany them vary greatly and are closely connected with the exercise of intelligence through consciousness. The individual has to choose ways of responding to his environment which are the most appropriate and most likely to gain the ends which he desires, and every decision which he makes will depend ultimately upon the evaluation of his feelings about the factors involved. The more intelligent he is the more quickly he is likely to perceive these factors, but in the end it will be his feelings about them that will be decisive. Thus it is that while intelligence may help to assess experience and to make use of its results, the springs of action are essentially emotional.

As the years of life pass, certain habitual ways of response to situations develop, many of them having been acquired in childhood. These include such things as the ways of dealing with success or failure, the capacities formed for loving and hating, trusting and suspecting, accepting or rejecting people. Modification is, of course, possible, but it is not simply a matter of intelligence or reason. It involves as well the extent to which new emotional responses can be developed, with their attendant risks of new and perhaps painful adjustments. Sometimes a person will make little adjustment to his emotional predicament throughout the whole of his life, especially if the predicament troubles him constantly with the shadow or threat of far off and barely remembered times.

The contribution of modern psychiatry is to help to explain these emotions at depth. In the past they were regarded almost entirely on a conscious level, though it was realised that a subconscious existed from which past experiences could be recalled. Now the unconscious is regarded as by far the most important sector of man's mental and moral life, as well as being the source of what is achieved in human character and activity.

This newly discovered unconscious is a realm of the psychic being in which willing and a kind of thinking goes on more or less independently of waking consciousness, but powerfully influencing bo'h the state of mind and the outward behaviour of the individual. Though far more is known about the unconscious today than in earlier times, it is still somewhat of a puzzle. But two things are more or less certain. The first is that it thinks in a way which is different from conscious thinking, since its ideas are expressed in images, symbols and snatches of dramatic presentation rather than in words. Secondly the complexes around which much of psychic energy is always revolving express the vital problems of the person's adaptation to life and often reveal themselves in dreams.

The explanation for this, which Sigmund Freud offered, was a biological one. Since unconscious phenomena always seem to express a tension, urgency or striving, his solution was the sexual instinct, which when working normally would maintain a balance in life. But the rejection or loss of the disciplinary influence of the father, or a failure to outgrow dependence upon the fostering love of the mother might lead to difficulties. It was therefore sexual experiences, especially in the first years of life, which Freud emphasised. Thus, for him, human relationships tended to be subordinated to instinctual satisfactions. An individual would seek contact with another basically to satisfy an organic need, arising out of chemical tensions. He tended to be an organism rather than a person.

One of Freud's chief colleagues, Alfred Adler, who became one of his notable opponents, also derived his notions from biology. But he was interested in growth and structure rather than in the generative problems of organism, and particularly in the way that living organisms strive to make good any defect or lesion in their structure. His view was that many, if not most, of the successful adaptations to life can be traced to a consistent striving to overcome what had been felt as an inferiority in childhood. Therefore he is often described as the psychologist of the will to power, though he insisted that power could only be a healthy aim if the individual knew what he wanted, and provided that he pursued his goal in harmony with the needs and aspirations of the community. He felt that it was just as important to investigate a person's attitude to society and to work, as it was to discover his real attitude to sex. Therefore his way of helping a person was to bring back into consciousness the motives behind his schemes for living and to help him to revalue these in the light of a more mature outlook. Thus while the followers of Freud were more interested in discovering any circumstances or shock in early life that may have blocked the normal course of a person's development, Adlerians, though they take account of a person's previous history and memories, look first for the present misuse of the psyche and what the subject imagines he is gaining from it.

Jung was far less specific than either Freud or Adler and maintained that behind these impulses to love and obtain gratification through loving and the urge to achieve power there was a fundamental force which was mysterious and indefinable, but virtually limitless in its possibilities. This he called 'the religious instinct', which could be cultivated and was of great use in helping a person to reach maturity. Roman Catholic writers, such as Father Victor White, have made much use of this idea.

Jung had two other concepts which are useful in trying to understand human behaviour. One is his theory of the structure of human personality which will be considered later in this chapter, and the other his analysis of the unconscious. Since his studies were anthropological as well as psychological, he had become interested in certain widespread myths which formed a part of the background of culture and civilisation. From these he evolved the idea that beneath the individual area of unconscious mental experience there existed a wider reservoir shared in the first instance by all members of any self-contained group, and this he called the racial unconscious. Deeper still, and in some way shared by the unconscious mind of every human being there lay a common pool of all human mental life, the universal unconscious. The existence of the 'collective unconscious', as these two deepest layers are often called, can be inferred in the normal man from the obvious traces of mythology in his dreams, but is even more apparent in the mythological imagery found with certain kinds of mental disorder.

Karen Horney is another critic of Freud, and her writings are useful to the laymen because they are almost entirely free of technical language. *The Neurotic Personality of Our Times* and *Our Inner Conflicts* both emphasise the importance of the individual's social and cultural background and the need to consider this when trying to understand his behaviour. Normality or abnormality can only be determined when we consider the culture within which the individual is functioning. There is no such thing as a universal normal way of behaviour, for all behaviour must be placed in its social and cultural background. There are, however, two traits which are present in all those tending to become neurotic; a rigidity in reaction and a discrepancy between potentialities and accomplishments.

Although psychologists differ in their emphasis with regard to the reasons for the ways in which people behave, and most counsellors are familiar with these differences, there are a number of relatively concrete and established mental processes which are commonly found in us all. They are related to the unconscious and to the ways in which unconscious matter may be recalled and brought within consciousness.

A simple way of defining consciousness is to say that it is the experience of being aware, and the content of consciousness is the sum of everything of which a person is aware at any given moment of time. Everything of this nature cannot possibly be in the mind of a person, especially when he is concentrating hard upon something else but it can fairly easily be recalled. Thus there is a pre-conscious area of the mind, which is a very large area indeed, wherein much of what is remembered is stored and available for recall when wanted. Ideas tend to be associated in many different ways, but depend upon fairly simple principles which form the basis for the whole process of learning and remembering. This wide network of associations provides innumerable links between one idea and another, and is set into motion when something is sought for in the memory.

But much of the forgotten material, while still present in the minds of adults, has passed not simply beyond their capacity to recall at will, but even beyond their capacity to remember that it had ever existed. The area where the material is deposited is the unconscious, and this is by no means a passive area. It contains not only the more primitive drives and impulses which may influence a person without his ever becoming fully aware of them, but also a number of extremely important constellations of ideas with a strong emotional quality which have at one time been present in the consciousness but which are no longer available to it. These constellations of ideas which are associated with strong feelings in a person's mind are known as complexes, and the process whereby a complex becomes buried in the unconscious part of the mind is called a repression.

The way in which this happens is the following. When an emotion, connected with a particular complex, reaches an unbearable degree of intensity the automatic defence of the individual's mind calls for one or both of two processes. The first is suppression, which involves the deliberate refusal to think about something extremely painful; if this is not enough to secure a temporary respite and the person's painful emotions are too insistent so that they tend to threaten the person's mental integrity, then repression takes place. But whereas suppression is a conscious act on the part of the individual, repression may take place without his ever having been aware of it.

The most common reasons for repression are that the material repressed has become charged with feelings either of intense guilt or of intense fear and anxiety. When a complex is stirred by some event in the conscious experience of an individual which has similar associations to those of the complex, the effect produced will be the reproduction of emotions resembling those which caused the complex, and these will probably be highly unpleasant and unbearable. A powerful mechanism, which Freud called 'the censorship', may then come into play, which will prevent the spontaneous reappearance of such material into consciousness. The unpleasant feelings will be aroused but the person will remain completely unaware of their source.

Compensatory mechanisms may then appear, usually in the form of rationalisation or projection. In the first of these processes some simple, convenient and ready-to-hand explanation is produced and accepted. It may have no connection at all with the real reason, but is a possible explanation for the situation. In the second the disagreeable experience is attributed to some acceptable scapegoat, which again will have no actual relationship with the situation. Both these processes can be entirely conscious to the person concerned, or they can be entirely unconscious. They can also be obvious to other people, or the deception which they are practising can be as convincing to others as it is to the individual involved. Situations like these are always present to a greater or lesser extent, and they will without doubt affect the behaviour of the individual concerned as well as his relationships with other people. But they may also result from such painful and powerful complexes, and produce such deep anxiety and depression that when allied to some constitutional or hereditary factor in the personality or body of the person concerned they may lead to mental illness. A person's make-up will have some appreciable effect upon such situations. It is therefore useful to know something about different types of personality structure and their susceptibility.

It is nearly 2,000 years ago since the Greek physician, Galen, tried to distinguish four fundamental temperamental differences, the sanguinic, the phlegmatic, the choleric and the melancholic, and various other classifications have been made since then. A more recent one is that of Kretschmer, who in his book *Physique and Character*, indicates certain biogenetic correlations in nature which enable one to discern and describe some typical patterns of physique which are apt to be associated with corresponding types of normal temperament and with certain psychopathic variants of that temperament. Similarly, Frank Lake in his *Clinical Theology* relates personality types to their disposition to various forms of mental illness. But for the more general use of the counsellor the personality types that Jung describes are adequate, and although they are criticised on the grounds that few people will fall exactly within these types, they do avoid the danger to the unwary of linking medical terms with certain fairly usual ways of behaviour.

Jung's conception of the structure of human personality is based upon the essential antithesis of thinking and feeling, and of sensation and intuition, in their contributions to personal experience. He divides the basic attitude of man to his existence into two opposite tendencies, introversion and extroversion. Introversion is concerned with subjective experience, with the person's own mental processes and the world of his thoughts and fantasies. Extroversion implies a predominant interesting objective experience in the external world of appearances and outside reality. Introversion means a great deal more than introspection. The introvert is not merely occupied with himself, but he is concerned with the meaning below the surface of things and with the nature of reality rather than with its visible and possible superficial appearance. Jung holds that both these tendencies exist in all people, but where the conscious attitude is one of introversion, the unconscious tendency will be towards extroversion, and vice versa.

The extroverted type is characterised by an outward flow of energy, an interest in events, in people and in things, a relationship with and a dependence upon them. This type is motivated by outside factors and is greatly influenced by his environment. He is sociable and confident in unfamiliar situations, on good terms with the world, and when he does not agree with people he prefers to argue or quarrel, or he tries to reshape things according to his own pattern. The introvert, on the other hand, tends to withdraw within himself, his feelings flow inwards, and he tends not to show them. He lacks confidence in relation to other people, is often unsociable, and he prefers reflection to activity.

These differences in attitude often seem to begin very early in childhood, and are sometimes thought to be innate. Both introverted and extroverted children are to be found in the same family and this helps to temper each other's tendencies. The extroverted child is the one who is popular both with parents and teachers. He is regarded as well adjusted and is often considered as more intelligent than he actually is. This is because of his early development and the good impression that he makes. The introverted child is shy and hesitant, dislikes new situations and approaches them with caution and sometimes fear. He prefers to play alone and have one rather than several friends. He is thoughtful and reflective, and often has a rich imaginative life. He has gifts but is slow in developing them, and takes time to feel at home in the world.

The adult who is extroverted is sociable, meets others halfway and is interested in practically everything. He likes organising groups, going to community gatherings and to parties, and he is usually active and helpful. He enjoys nothing more than an audience, dislikes being alone and thinks reflection morbid. This makes him more attractive to those on the outer world than to his family and immediate circle who often find him bumptious and overpowering. His weaknesses lie in a tendency to superficiality, a dependence on making a good impression and a lack of self-criticism. Since he is well adapted to society, he usually accepts its morals and conventions and so tends to be rather orthodox in his attitudes and judgements.

On the other hand, the introverted adult dislikes social activities, and feels lonely and lost in large gatherings. He is sensitive and afraid of looking ridiculous. He prefers reading to noisy activities, and his own thought to conversation and he regards his judgements as more important than the generally accepted opinions. He usually keeps his best qualities to himself and only shows them in sympathetic and intimate surroundings. So he is often undervalued and may in some circumstances be less successful than his extroverted colleague.

Jung makes further distinctions within these groups according to the four functions which he considers are used by people to orientate themselves to the world. The first of these is thinking, which gives meaning and understanding to what a person does.

The second is feeling, which weighs and values things. The third is sensation, or perception through the senses, and the fourth intuition which tells of future possibilities and gives a person information of the atmosphere which surrounds all experience. Feeling is sometimes confused with emotion, while in fact any of these functions can lead to emotion, so that emotion is itself an expression of one or other of these functions.

The thinking type is an individual whose actions are usually the result of an intellectually considered motive. If he is an extroverted thinker he thinks things out and comes to conclusions based on objective data, or facts. He likes logic and order and invents neat formulae to express his views. He believes that these formulae represent the absolute truth, and so it becomes a moral duty to press their claims. He thinks that he is logical and rational, but in fact he suppresses all that does not fit into his schemes, or refuses to recognise it. Since he dislikes and fears the irrational, he is singularly cold and lacking in human relationships. He can sacrifice his friends and family to his principles without any idea that he is doing so, and he may become a family tyrant. Since he represses emotion and feeling, this tends to burst out at times with a violence which is quite beyond his control. Therefore he is the type who may have affairs with unsuitable women and cause distress to those he loves. Similarly he may often suffer from irrational moods which he rarely admits, and doubts about his beliefs which he stifles with fanaticism. His strong sense of duty and purpose for his life will contain much that is good, but will lack human qualities, particularly warmth and tolerance.

The introverted thinker is interested in ideas rather than in facts, and his value lies in the new ideas and views which he brings to things. But he is concerned with his ideas as an addition to knowledge rather than in their use. Like the extroverted thinker he is lacking in human qualities and is often unconscious of what is going on. He does not understand how people think or feel and so he is either shy or silent when in the company of others, or when he does speak he will often make the most inappropriate remark.

The feeling person is completely different to the thinking. He is very interested in human relationships and with the value or lack of value of people, and their ways of behaviour to each other. The extroverted feeling type is well adjusted to the world, is deeply interested in personal relationships, has tact, and charm, is accomplished at smoothing out awkward situations, and at pouring oil on troubled waters. When he becomes aware of real unhappiness or injustice, he has an overpowering desire to help, and is much sought after in social and community life.

The introverted feeling type gives the impression of coldness, but since he does not express his feelings, they are often intensely strong. He is not demonstrative, but has much sympathy and understanding when anyone is in trouble or need, and so he makes a constant and reliable friend. Such feeling may express itself in religion, in poetry or music, and on rare occasions in an outstanding act of self-sacrifice.

Sensation differs from feeling in that it is confined to what reaches a person through his senses. When the type is extroverted the object arousing the sensation is the important thing. The person of this type takes everything as it comes, experiences things as they actually are, does not try to look deeper into them or to alter them in his imagination. Such people are easy, jolly and have a great capacity for enjoyment. Their main danger lies in overvaluing the senses, and so they may turn into luxury-loving and restless pleasure-seekers.

The introverted sensation type is concerned principally with experiencing the sensation. Such people include artists and musicians and all those who are engaged in creative expression. They are often overwhelmed by the impressions which they get, and need time to assimilate them. They may think they see people who are not really there and they are often preoccupied with images and archetypes from the collective unconscious.

Intuition, like sensation, is an irrational function. It perceives realities which are not necessarily known to the consciousness. But it does so for a creative purpose and so may often try to alter a situation to make it come within the range of the vision.

The extroverted intuitive regards all important things as possibilities. Neither religion nor law is sacrosanct when he is on the trail of something, and people's feelings or convictions are sacrificed when need be. The tendency for this type of person is to squander his possessions and never to reap the reward. For it is almost impossible for him to carry a thing through, beyond the point where success is established. Thus his personal relationships are very weak, he finds it difficult to stick to wife or friend, and yet life with him is never dull.

The introverted intuitive is the type who sees visions, has revelations of a religious type, prophetic dreams or weird fantasies. He is often regarded as peculiar, if not mad, which he can actually become if he cannot find a way to relate his experiences to life. Usually he keeps quiet about these things, and so seems rather odd and strange, or he may join a little group or esoteric sect which is interested in such experiences.

The extent to which these different types are accepted in society depends very much on the nature of the culture to which they belong, and the value which a particular culture places upon their attributes. Our society gives far greater prestige to the thinking type than it usually does to the others, and this often gives the false impression of superiority to people of this type. It also expects different characteristics in its men and women. Women are thought to be biased towards the feeling types, and perhaps the intuitive. In actual fact, this is due more to environmental, educational and situational reasons than to actual differences in make-up.

Since it is very rare to find the absolutely pure type the value of this sort of classification of personality could be questioned. Even Jung refers to his classification of types as 'somewhat Galtonesque family portraits' for human nature cannot be classified in a precise and simple way. But this concept of types has great practical value as an aid to understanding personal relationships. It enables a person to realise that another person may think and act in quite a different way under similar circumstances, and it guides a counsellor in his anticipation of the behaviour of someone he is helping.

It is very common among maladjusted people to find that they have developed one function to a very great extent so that the others are neglected. For example, the intuitive can so neglect sensation that he takes little care of his health, and the thinking type can entirely overlook personal relationships and find himself in serious personal difficulties. Help for such people involves the development of the neglected functions so that the personality can become more nearly whole.

The secure and well adjusted individual will usually have reached a workable balance between these different functions. But when he is faced with some sudden insecurity, danger or threat a profound change may take place in this balance. Thus a person who is fairly well integrated may become aggressive or weakly compliant in such a situation. But this will only be temporary and he will return to his usual self when the danger is past or absorbed. The ordinary person will be able, in a very short time, to adjust himself to some unexpected event, like the birth of another child, promotion at work, an accident, an illness or death in the family. But if the personality is not well adjusted the change may be lasting, or it may present a complete barrier which the person cannot cross. It then becomes a matter for the psychotherapist rather than the counsellor.

These different types of people will deal in different ways with the various 'ups and downs' of life. But when things are not going as well as they should anxiety will usually prevail. Anxiety is the keynote in the psychological approach to human problems. It disturbs a sense of peace in the individual; it leads to organic tension and is the root cause of neurosis. It can distort the development of character, cause an active self-centredness in a person, and a preoccupation with aches and pains, rights and wrongs, prospects and misfortunes, which are often regarded as selfishness. The unrecognised projection of deep-seated anxiety and fear on to neighbours or on to external circumstances can be the cause of a great deal of unhappiness to people, while basic anxiety invades many aspects of life – the home, politics, business, sport, and even religion. It is only the few, fully mature people who succeed in living above the anxiety common to us all, and most people find an attitude of adventure and faith which such living demands extremely difficult.

Fear differs from anxiety in being the conscious reaction, or painful emotion, which occurs with impending danger, and it is proportionate to the danger which has to be faced. The decision as to whether danger exists depends upon the knowledge prevalent in the particular culture. Thus primitive peoples will fear many things which a more sophisticated society understands. On the other hand a knowledgeable society may discover many other things to fear.

Anxiety always expresses a disproportionate reaction to danger, or even a reaction to imaginary danger. It is a long drawn out state of apprehension, proportionate to the meaning which a particular situation has for the person concerned, and the reasons why he is so anxious are often unknown to him. Since anxiety concerns not only the situation as it stands in reality, but the situation as it appears to a particular individual, methods of persuasion to try to argue a person out of his anxiety may be quite useless. The therapeutic task is, therefore, to find out the meaning of a certain situation to the person concerned, which may involve delving into the unconscious as well as into the conscious.

Although each individual has special things over which he tends to be anxious, the crucial conflicts around which anxiety grows are likely to be the same. There are certain typical difficulties inherent in our culture which mirror themselves as conflicts in every individual life and which, when accumulated, may develop into deep anxiety. In a competitive society such as ours there is always the conflict between success and brotherly love and humility, which is particularly relevant to the Christian who is told to follow the latter and yet finds it very hard to eschew the former. Then there is the artificial stimulation of our needs by all possible forms of advertisement and the fact that in most cases it is impossible to satisfy them in the ways suggested. For the individual this means a constant discrepancy between his desires and their fulfilment. Lastly there is the alleged freedom of the individual as the basis of his philosophy of living, and the factual limitations which he experiences in his life. People do not necessarily frame their conflicts in this way, but they appear in such forms as jealousy between friends, fears of personal failure, feelings of inferiority, and of entire helplessness.

Many of the communal and cultural sources of anxiety today lie in the rapid changes which are taking place in society to which it is very difficult to adjust, especially in the later years of life. A person with too set a mind in the modern world tends to run the risk of being broken by it. Far more than we realise, we depend for our emotional support on a fairly stable material basis and a relatively undisturbed routine of life. Change, particularly threatened change, brings about an inner unrest which drives people into uncooperative and selfish actions and attitudes. They tend to adopt an attitude of self-assertion, aggressiveness and shrewdness which is quite out of proportion to the needs of the situation; and fail to develop their sensitivity and sentimentality which would help them to adjust themselves.

Anxiety can be escaped in a variety of ways. It is possible to rationalise a fear, and so to turn anxiety into some definite threat which can then be dealt with. It is possible to deny the existence of a fear, and then either to become reckless, or to suffer some of the physical concomitants of repression, such as strain, fatigue and exhaustion which are quite disproportionate with any physical tiredness. Some people narcotise anxiety with alcohol or drugs, with constant social activity for fear of being alone, with an ordinate desire for sleep, with sexual activities, or even with excessive work. Others avoid all situations in which anxious thought or feelings may arise. They then stand the risk of inhibitions such as inability to do, feel, or think certain things, or in their extreme form, of paralysis of a limb, blindness or speechlessness.

Since our culture generates a great deal of anxiety, practically everyone has built up one or other of these defences to a greater or a lesser extent. The more disturbed a person is, the more is his personality pervaded by such defences and the greater the number of things he is unable to do, or does not consider doing, although according to his vitality, his natural capacities, or his educational background he is capable of doing these things. The more severe the disturbance the more inhibitions there are likely to be present, and the less conscious he is of them.

The answer to the problem of fear and anxiety for the normally healthy mind is a positive philosophy of life, or what the Christian would designate as a state of faith. This makes personal effort worthwhile and gives a pattern of meaning to the ups and downs of life. But to the person verging on neurosis, or to the neurotic himself, it is useless. His utter irrationality and complete helplessness makes him unable to overhaul and to challenge what he fears within himself. He needs the help of the trained understanding of a psychotherapist which will bring to light his unconscious fears and anxieties, and in the process of doing so will help him to cope with them.

Neurotic anxieties or fears differ both in quality and quantity from those which are normal to the prevailing cultural pattern.

They are more pervasive and far deeper than the ordinary run of anxieties. The protective devices of customs and rites do not touch them, and the normal ways of dealing with them mean little to the sufferer. The individual undergoing such an anxiety has the feeling of a powerful, inescapable danger against which he is entirely helpless. The condition that is fostered is an all-pervading feeling of being lonely and unprotected in a hostile world.

The cause for this may be entirely circumstantial and the result of an accumulation of difficulties which have arrived together or on top of one another. This was often the reason for the neurosis which developed during war time. It is what Karen Horney calls 'situation neurosis' and it yields fairly easily to therapeutic treatment. 'Character neurosis' on the other hand is far deeper, and usually shows itself in a basic form of anxiety which is more or less similar in all cases, though varying in extent and intensity. It is a feeling of being small, insignificant, helpless, deserted and endangered in a world 'that is out to abuse, cheat, attack, humiliate, betray and envy'. Such a person needs to shield himself from the world, and he does so quite often by an inordinate craving for affection, or for power, prestige and possessions.

All human beings suffer to some extent from the frustrations which arise from conflict and anxiety, and with help most are able to make an appropriate adjustment. Counselling is intended to give that help which all of us require at times in our lives, so that we may be able, with our varied types of personality, to meet the demands of life. But when the frustration leads to a retreat or a flight from real life, then far more skilled help is needed.

Both psychotherapy and counselling provide this sort of understanding of a person, though psychotherapy delves deeper into the unconscious and the collective unconscious, while counselling confines itself to the conscious and to things which can be easily recalled. Likewise, the methods of both are similar,

A NEW UNDERSTANDING OF PEOPLE

but although counselling is aware of the deeper needs of the personality it does not try to deal with them.

There are several important ways in which a knowledge of psychotherapy can help the counsellor. In the first place, it can offer hypotheses concerning the influence of past experience on present behaviour and so give some idea as to the ways in which unconscious feelings influence behaviour. This permits a deeper understanding of the problems involved. It can also enable the counsellor to envisage a more realistic plan for helping the person to deal with his difficulties. Thus some knowledge of psychotherapy is essential to the counsellor for his own use, but it is also needful to enable him to decide when the needs of a person are beyond his powers, and when it is necessary for him to refer the person to a medically trained psychiatrist.

IV. The Basic Principles of Counselling

In the past those in the helping services tended to deal with problems. People with material needs were usually in the care of the welfare worker. People whose problems seemed to spring from their mental make-up were often helped by the caseworker. The particular needs of children and of the old, of those on probation, or the person in hospital or in prison were each looked after by some specialised social worker. The clergy dealt with those who had religious problems, the teacher with educational problems and the doctor with medical problems.

These problems still exist and need to be dealt with as such, but more often than not there is some underlying cause or some difficulty in personality or in human relationships of which the problem is a symptom. In fact it often happens that when a problem is removed or solved, the personality is not necessarily more integrated. The trouble will merely change its nature and break out in some other form. Social workers are often finding this with people who drift from one agency to another, seemingly obtaining help in some particular respect, but in fact never getting any nearer to being able to cope on their own. What they really need is a deeper understanding of themselves and of the causes of their behaviour, and this is what counselling attempts to give them.

In trying to understand other people, it is essential to realise that everyone is unique. Classification into types can be useful in order to help with understanding, but nobody falls exactly in the same way into any of these types. Each of us looks at a situation through our own private pair of spectacles and these can reveal very different things. The first task of a would-be counsellor is to learn to know what the world looks like through spectacles other than his own. Only then will he find another person's feelings and behaviour intelligible, and so be able to choose some common ground on which to meet. It is through this sort of relationship that it becomes possible to gain an insight into the feelings and thoughts of others and so to discern a little about the problems that face another person.

Very rarely do two individuals respond in exactly the same way to help that is offered, even though their respective problems may seem to have much in common. Therefore the counsellor has to have a sensitive awareness in every instance of the kind of person with whom he is dealing. It is through the counselling relationship that it becomes possible to gain insight into the other person's feelings and thoughts and so to discover a little about his real self.

The very basis of counselling lies in the relationship between two people. This relationship is a continuous process through which one human being tries to help another by the methods which underlie the production of good human relations. As Father Biestek expresses it: 'With the motive of love, he (the counsellor) strives for skill in the use of the wisdom of science to help his brother in need.'[6]

This relationship is not just a giving of interest, friendship and understanding on the counsellor's part. It also leads to a response on the part of the person who comes for counselling. This in its turn should engender a new response from the counsellor, and so on. So that the relationship becomes a dynamic interaction between them, with changing but responsive attitudes and emotions as it deepens.

In these ways it is like all other good human relationships. But there are distinctions between the counselling relationship and other relationships. The equality and mutuality of a friend to friend relationship are absent, for although both are equal as human beings, the counsellor is always the person who is giving help, and the person himself is the one who is receiving it. It is also only a temporary relationship, for it lasts only so long as the counselling is needed and then is broken off.

Various terms have been applied to describe this relationship. Sympathy or empathy are commonly used: 'sympathy' emphasising the emotional component in a successful communication with another person, and 'empathy' indicating a rather more detached but deeper and more realistic sharing of feeling. 'Rapport' has been borrowed from psychology to try to give a more precise meaning to the so-called emotional bridge over which the factual data regarding the person and his problem will pass backwards and forwards with interpretation, enlightenment and guidance. But whatever term is used, the essence of the relationship is a dynamic interaction between the two persons for the benefit of the person who has come for help.

The idea of a dynamic relationship implies that the back and forth movement is continuous, though it may change direction and rate of speed. It will start with a movement from the person to the counsellor as the person reveals his problem and also himself. It will continue from the counsellor to the person through the sensitive understanding which the counsellor shows, however wordless this may be; and it is directed towards the counsellor again as he becomes aware of the counsellor's response and seeks to show that this is so, and perhaps to indicate other feelings and attitudes.

Pastoral counselling has a further dimension to add, since the counsellor seeks as well to strengthen the person's relationship with God. He does this as part of the counselling process, both through the knowledge that the person has of the counsellor's own faith, and also by the Christian interpretation that he will give when needed to his problems. The pastoral counsellor, unlike the caseworker, does not keep his beliefs to himself, but on the other hand he does not introduce them indiscriminately, but only as part of the counselling process and when the person is ready to receive them.

This dynamic relationship cannot take place without some expression of feeling; nor can it be successful unless there is some control over the emotional involvement. Every person is by nature a social being, with the need to communicate with other human beings, to express his thoughts, attitudes and feelings, and this need is especially felt when a person is in some kind of trouble or difficulty which intensifies the desire to share the burden with another person. Furthermore it is important that he should do so, for some expression of feeling is necessary not only to relieve the atmosphere, but also to make the person feel more able to take some positive constructive action. It helps to deepen the relationship between the person and the counsellor, and so to make it possible for a more adequate understanding of the person and his problem, and it also acts as a psychological support since the person will feel that his burden is lessened by sharing it with the counsellor.

The sort of conditions under which it is possible to express oneself freely is sometimes described as 'permissive'. The counsellor has to create an environment in which the person will feel comfortable in giving expression to his feelings, and this is far more important than anything that the counsellor can say. A permissive atmosphere is not easy to put into words. It can perhaps be regarded as one in which the person can express his thoughts in his own way, without any feeling that the counsellor will not understand, be shocked or condemn him for what he says. Everyone who comes to a counsellor does so with a certain amount of trepidation and the sooner the counsellor puts him at his ease, the less time they will take before they can both feel at one in their new relationship.

The counsellor also has something to contribute, and that is the real desire to help the person. In the beginning of each new relationship this desire has more of an intellectual element which is largely an awareness that this is a human being in trouble, asking and expecting some form of help. But as the relationship grows, this desire to help takes on more feeling tones, and there develops an understanding of the person and his problems on both an intellectual and emotional level, as well as a reaching out towards him. The counsellor begins to feel with the person, and the desire to help is conveyed through these feeling tones. Once feelings begin to be expressed, an emotional involvement starts, and it is up to the counsellor to decide the extent to which this shall be allowed to continue and the amount of control he should exercise.

In order to do this it is essential that he should undertsand the person to as great a degree as possible. To interpret the meaning of feelings or evoke a knowledge of human behaviour is indispensable and this knowledge comes partly from some study of psychology, psychiatry and the other social sciences as was indicated in the previous chapter, and also from introspection with regard to one's own life and experiences and some consideration of the experiences of others. This knowledge becomes a framework within which this particular person, with his individual and unique qualities, can be understood and helped.

It also requires a sensitivity which is able to see behind much of what is being expressed and so to discover the real purpose and motives of the feelings aroused. Sensitivity itself is a gift which benefits by usage, but it can be acquired to a surprising extent through a real conviction on the counsellor's part about the importance of feelings in a person's life, and a determined effort to discover what these feelings are. Lack of sensitivity is often due to the inability of the counsellor to control his own feelings and train of thought in an interview. He allows these to blind him to the currents of emotion which are discernible in the relationship.

In this continuous dynamic relationship, understanding and sensitivity are not sufficient in themselves. The counsellor has to respond so that the person feels able to release more emotions or feelings about his problem. This response has many forms, as will be seen in the next chapter, but it has meaning only as it 'comes from the heart', and is successful in conveying this to the person. Its immediate purpose may be to give psychological support by sympathetic listening and understanding; to strengthen the person's security in expressing his feelings; to help him to show progressively deeper feelings; or to encourage further expression. The important thing is that the response should be deliberate and with a definite purpose in mind. It has to be of such a nature that it calls forth necessary emotions, but exerts a control over them so that they do not block further progress or embarrass either the person or the counsellor.

When two people meet in this way the feelings aroused may not be only those of the immediate meeting and occasion, but they may be linked with former experience. The past may be being revived and lived in the present. In the course of analytical treatment Freud discovered that patients were experiencing towards him feelings that had formerly been experienced in their relationships with people who had been important to them in their early life. In other words these feelings were transferred to him from their original objects, and so he called such a situation 'transference'. In psychoanalysis patients are helped to re-live these early emotional experiences, so that they may become released from them. Work of this nature may require a deep understanding of the unconscious and its manifestations and the use of interpretative methods which are highly specialised. When this is the case it is outside the scope of the counsellor.

The counsellor, however, needs to recognise and understand such feelings and attitudes, even though he should not encourage the re-living of them. An understanding of them will help to explain why a person suddenly becomes over-demanding or extremely diffident, very fond of or very angry with the counsellor. Usually such feelings will be only temporary and will naturally pass away as counselling progresses. But sometimes it may be necessary to draw the person's attention to what is actually happening, and so to enable him to realise the meaning of these feelings and the elements of unreality and misconception which they hold.

This continuous and dynamic backwards and forwards relationship between the counsellor and the person he is helping is only possible when the value of the person is recognised and when the counsellor meets him on equal terms. This implies a respect for him and an acceptance of the 'whole' person. The counsellor sees the person as he really is, including his strength and his weaknesses, his congenial and his uncongenial qualities, his positive and his negative feelings, his constructive and his destructive attitudes and behaviour. And yet he maintains all the time a sense of the person's innate dignity and personal worth. It does not mean the approval of any deviant attitudes and behaviour. It means understanding the person as he is at that moment, and also understanding him at the different stages of change in attitude which he is likely to undergo in the process of counselling. Thus he should feel safe to reveal himself and look at himself as he really is, and so deal with his problem and himself in a more realistic manner.

The person who comes for counselling probably knows something of his own failure and weaknesses, but fears disapproval from the counsellor. He may bear some resentment against the conditions which make it necessary for him to come for counselling, and therefore he puts up his defences. The counsellor needs to recognise this, and be able to be glad that the person has come and feels able to express his feelings, rather than to resent anything which may be said.

A counsellor also needs to have a very good knowledge of himself and of his own attitudes and feelings if he is to find acceptance easy. He has to accept himself with his own faults, biases and prejudices, before he can help another to do the same.

This is particularly the case when he has some negative and undesirable attitudes which are similar to those of the person who has come to him for help. If he has not resolved his own conflicts, he will find it very difficult to help another to do so, and if there are things in his own life which he has not dealt with realistically, he will be quite unable to deal with them as realities in another person's life.

Furthermore, without an awareness of his own attitudes and feelings, he is liable to follow his natural tendency to impute his own feelings to the person he is counselling. He may mistakenly conclude that he knows what the person is feeling about a particular situation because he would feel the same. While, in fact, the person feels very differently. The counsellor will then not perceive reality as it is, and the person he is helping may feel this as a subtle form of rejection.

Even if he has resolved his own conflicts over something, there is always the possibility of recognising something in the person he is helping which is very akin to something in his own life, and responding emotionally in a way which meets his own needs rather than those of the person. This is sometimes called over-identification, and it can easily happen in the case of an injustice which the counsellor feels very strongly or some situation which is very like one in which the counsellor has found himself. Over-identification, from whatever motive, creates a blind spot in the counsellor and so impedes his perception of things as they are in reality and therefore endangers the effectiveness of the total helping process.

The most important thing of all is that the person shall not feel that the counsellor is losing respect for him because of something which he has revealed. If this does happen, the person begins to lose his sense of dignity and worth. It is in real love that the counsellor has to accept the person who comes to him, and this is a two-way relationship. Each is aware that he has weaknesses and strengths, successes and failures, and that in spite of these, possibly even because of them, mutual respect continues and even increases.

The result of this accepting attitude on the part of the counsellor is to make it possible for the person to become freer from tension and anxiety, and so to make it less necessary for him to protect himself from acknowledging his deeper feelings and attitudes, and the value they have for him. This, of course, will not remove them, but help him to face them more constructively. He will express what he really thinks and feels, without thought of what the counsellor wants to hear and the security of this relationship will permit him to reveal himself with his limitations and mistakes, without detriment to his inner sense of dignity.

Acceptance is particularly important, and often very difficult to offer, to the person who comes to a counsellor not looking for comfort or for some sort of help, but with a grudge, or with a sense of hostility about something that the counsellor has done or stands for. The natural attitude of the counsellor would be to become defensive, or to argue his case. Yet what helps the person most in this sort of situation is the experience of meeting someone who, even when he shows his unpleasant side, does not reject him. This may often be the first time that this has happened, and the shock can be so salutary that he will begin to look at himself, reassess the hurtful things in his life, and see himself more truly than ever before.

It is not only necessary to accept a person as such, but also to remember that he is a rational creature who can pursue reasonable ends in a reasonable way, even though he may be driven by strong internal or external forces. Like every human being, he has the responsibility of living his life in such a manner as to achieve his own ends as he conceives them and to decide the appropriate means for attaining his own personal destiny. The exercise of this responsibility is one of the principal sources of personality growth and development and only by making free choices can the person strive towards maturity in the intellectual, social, emotional and spiritual aspects of his personality.

The counsellor has to help him to see his problem or need clearly and in perspective. This means helping him to work through the emotional disturbance which the problem has created and which has deprived him of the clarity of seeing himself and the problem properly. He has to help the person to free himself from the fears and tensions which he has acquired in order to release his dormant resources. He has to create a relationship in which the person can grow and work out his own problem, move along at his own speed and in his own way.

What the counsellor should not do is to allow the person to play only a subordinate role in all this and so himself to assume the principal responsibility for working out the problem. He should not manœuvre the person to choose or decide in such a way that he is not fully aware of the process or feels that he is being moved about against his will. Nor should he persuade in a controlling way, so that the person feels that he is in a subordinate role of only participating or co-operating. He needs to go slowly and carefully, at the person's own pace, supporting him at each stage, and helping him to make his own choice when a suitable moment arrives.

This approach, which may be called one of self-determination, has its limits. A person cannot be completely free to choose and decide as he likes. The rights of one individual are circumscribed by those of other individuals in society. Nor can a person have rights without also having duties. These rights and duties are defined partly by law, and partly by a wide range of moral and social customs. A counsellor has to make a person aware of these, and help him to direct his choices in a manner which does not conflict with them. But this does not necessarily mean an authoritarian approach which tells the person exactly what he ought to do. It means being sure that he knows the accepted legal or moral attitude of the community, but leaving him free to make his own decision.

The capacity for making positive and constructive decisions varies greatly from person to person, and the counsellor has to be aware of this, and not force the need for self-determination beyond the person's capacity for it. The evaluation of this capacity is one of the more difficult of the counsellor's skills, but it is also one of the most important. He should assume that the person is capable of making his own constructive plans and decisions until he is convinced that this is not the case. It may be that a person passes through times in the process of counselling when some support is needed, or when some help in making up his mind about the next step is required. Another person may not have a capacity for positive and constructive decision making. Either he is too weak to assume full responsibility for the direction of his own situation, and then he will need some supportive help. Or he may have deep-seated emotional difficulties, or firmly fixed character disorders and then he is beyond the help of the counsellor. It is important to recognise this at a fairly early stage, or the person may think that the counsellor has failed, and is just handing him on to someone else.

Recently, a far greater attention has been paid to the ways in which the personality is able to maintain its own integrity and foster its own growth, and this is sometimes referred to as ego-psychology. Freud distinguished between the id, the ego and the super-ego in the personality. The id he regarded as the unconscious reserve of primitive instincts which are responsible for the behaviour of the new-born child. As the child comes to terms with external reality and begins to make his own decisions a part of this becomes separated off and differentiated as the ego or self. Its main function is to bring about some sort of co-ordination in this seething mass of impulses or instinctual drives. At a still later stage in the child's development there arises, out of the need to adjust to society's moral prohibitions the super-ego, which is loosely equated with the conscience but may actually resemble it very little. In the past those counselling others con-

THE BASIC PRINCIPLES OF COUNSELLING 65

centrated either upon helping them to relax the over-exacting standards of their super-ego and to release some of their repressed sexual and aggressive feelings or to strengthen an inadequate super-ego. Now the emphasis is upon the ego itself and its work of integrating the personality.

According to recent American thought, the ego is an integrative mechanism whose usual function is not to defend itself against the instincts in its main purpose of dealing with anxiety in the personality, but rather to learn how it can satisfy the needs of the organism. Even when it is confronted with a conflict, its primary task is to try to find a solution, rather than to defend itself against recognising the conflict, or having to engage in a struggle with it. Therefore, for practical purposes this new emphasis recognises the importance of studying a person's own problem-solving apparatus and ability, and regarding the person as one who is able to do this rather than one who has to be enabled.

The general process of counselling should help to strengthen the ego of the person. As discussion takes place the need for repression will be lessened. Feelings of anxiety, inadequacy and defeat will be reduced as they are expressed, and the counsellor can often help by reassurance, and by suggesting something for the person to do, in which he is likely to succeed. Thus, step by step, sometimes without the actual realisation that this is happening, the person will be gaining a greater power to mould his own life.

A particular concern of the counsellor is to help the person see more clearly the nature of outer reality and his own relationship to it. Unrealistic outlooks and attitudes are often at the root of his troubles, and the counsellor has to help him to see them in the light of his own real life experiences. Relationships, attitudes and beliefs that are unrecognised are often handicapping the person and when these can be realised the person is in a position to adapt or change them to meet the needs of reality. But it is the person himself who needs to do this, as he gradually recognises his unrealistic approach, and as his ego becomes strong enough to cope with change.

Counsellors are sometimes sceptical of the effectiveness of treatment which does not go to the psychological roots of the problems of emotional adjustment, and are too concerned with cure and too little interested in improving, even by a little, a person's capacity for a satisfying and useful life. Although in many cases the more thoroughgoing help would be to strengthen the basic character structure, this is often not possible. The person may be too old to benefit from such therapy, or more usually there may not be the facilities, the time or the finances available. The counsellor can help to carry the person over the period of crisis and enable him to achieve at least his former level of competency.

The way a person meets life is the sum total of all his past and present experiences and is the result of a slow educative process carried on throughout the whole of his life. This may not have led to an ideal adjustment, and there may be many things which could have been done better, but in most cases there is no real necessity to dig into the personality in order to bring about what seems a more suitable adjustment. The counsellor's job is to do what he can to further the process of adjustment and to create greater freedom for the person to gain a truer perception of the outside world and of his powers for relating to it.

Environmental pressures can be as important as emotional pressures in leading to some of the difficulties brought to the counsellor. The term 'environment' refers to a very large range of phenomena and will include the large and small social groups with which the person may come into contact, groups such as the local church or club, his membership of social institutions like the family, and the culture of the whole society and its subgroups of which he forms part. In each of these the person has a role to play. He may be unaware of what exactly his role is, he may be unable for some reason to play it properly, or he may be in the process of changing his role and finding it difficult to do so.

The counsellor needs to know this, and his knowledge comes from observation, and perhaps from a little discreet private enquiry. It is usually possible from manner and dress to get some idea of social class. An address, which is a normal and acceptable question to ask, will reveal something of the neighbourhood and its type of culture. Family membership, occupation and interests are likely to come up in the course of conversation. To the counsellor all these things are not just incidental, but they are the means whereby he may form a picture of the environment from which the person comes.

At the same time as he is doing this, he is also trying to discover whether the person feels that he fits into the roles which he is expected to follow. The person himself may give some indication of this by the way he describes the people with whom he mixes, or the difficulties which he encounters. But often it is what he does not mention which is relevant, and this can only be discovered when the counsellor has a very good knowledge of different types of environment and of the areas in which the persons he is helping are likely to live. He has to picture to himself the type of person and his contacts, the sort of reception he is likely to invoke and his flexibility in changing his role to suit the company which he happens to be in.

The counsellor may sometimes be able to interpret the environment to the person and so make it easier for him to fit in. Or he may be able to suggest some ways in which the person can adapt his role to feel more at home in his environment. The counsellor's help is particularly needed when a person finds difficulty in altering his way of life, and this will happen at times such as the death of a near relative, or some permanent illness or handicap. It will happen, too, at the different stages in life, when a person realises that he is now middle-aged or old and no longer retains the status or position in a group which he previously held. It can also happen with a change in job or rapid promotion. Great tact and sensitivity to the person are required, and although advice may be needed it is necessary to be very careful in giving it, and to do so in a way which will make the person feel that it comes as the result of his own prompting rather than as counsel from someone else.

Many of the problems related to environmental pressure which come the way of the counsellor also contain some emotional content, and so have to be tackled from both sides at once. The counsellor has to try to lessen the external difficulties and at the same time build up the personal capacity to deal with them. Similarly emotional problems are rarely present without some environmental difficulty and when this is reduced the individual is often more able to face reality as it is. The counsellor has to be aware of both these aspects of the problems that are brought to him, and by dealing with them both is better able to strengthen the person so that he can use his own capacities to work out for himself a life which is both satisfying to himself and useful to society.

V. Counselling in Action

In the counselling interview the counsellor works at two levels. At one level there is the nature of the problem which the person brings to the counsellor, the meaning of it to himself and how he is reacting to the circumstances at the moment both in his own surroundings and at the interview itself. Underlying this is the person himself, what manner of individual he is, what sort of life experience he has had and how he has reacted to it. At each of the different stages of counselling, when the person is relating his problems, when he is gradually gaining insight into them, and when he is thinking out some sort of solution, the relationship has to be carried on at both these levels. This is by no means easy to do, but it is essential if the person is to be helped to become more mature and more of a real person.

The ordinary person will only go to a counsellor when he is unable to find a solution himself, and this may be when he is at the end of his tether. He will rarely feel like telling the counsellor everything, and in fact he will be assessing the counsellor and deciding, as a result of this assessment, just how much he feels he can say, and even whether it is worth his while coming to another interview if this were to be suggested. Therefore very much depends upon the initial contact with the counsellor and how he meets the person who is coming to consult him.

The counsellor has to try to convey warmth in his reception so that the person feels that he is in the presence of someone who will listen carefully and with sympathy and that his problems can be unfolded without fear of blame or misunderstanding. In this way a relationship can come into being which makes him feel free to tell his own story in his own way and at his own pace.

The physical setting of the interview may determine its entire potentiality. This starts when the interview is arranged and may depend upon how the telephone is answered when he summons up enough courage to decide to seek help. He may be phoning from a call box and find its method of working difficult to understand, and by the time he gets through he may have reached such a state of tension that he is quite incoherent. Patience and sympathy will help him to pull himself together. If he writes, then a warm and courteous letter asking him to call will do much to put him at his ease. Sudden demands for help sometimes occur, and however fictitious the reason may seem, it is rarely wise to refuse, for so often the immediate request is a cover for something far deeper.

The manner of greeting him when he arrives can be of great importance, for he will probably have had to pull himself together in order to come. He may have to await his turn and this can be a very painful business especially if his decision to come may only just have outweighed all the reasons against. Reading and pictorial matter can help, but often a personal word of sympathy and understanding as an explanation of the delay will enable him to wait more calmly.

Some degree of privacy and a comfortable relaxed atmosphere are important. Interruptions and telephone calls should be reduced to a minimum so that the counsellor can devote the whole of his attention to the person coming to him for help. A pleasant and friendly greeting will enable them to become acquainted at once. Comfort and relaxation is most likely to build up this relationship and so an easy chair is to be preferred to a hard one and a talk round the fire to a discussion across a desk. For if a person is going to talk about things which he would rather not reveal to someone he does not yet know, the sooner he can feel at ease the better the interview will proceed.

It is always difficult to know how to start an interview. Sometimes the person himself may help by pouring out his troubles, but more often he may hesitate, not knowing what to say, and perhaps say nothing at all. It is not usually desirable to talk about the weather or some topical subject, as would be the case in a social meeting, for it is very diffcult to change this type of conversation and to move from the impersonal to the personal. Something about the person who comes, his appearance, his attitude or his gestures may suggest his purpose of coming, and a welcome given in a questioning manner may help him to start talking, and this is always preferable to the counsellor having to decide how to start.

The initial aim of the counsellor is to make a dialogue possible with the person, and this means getting on to the same wavelength so that each can understand the other. The counsellor has to identify himself with the person so that he can view what the person tells him in the same way as the person views it; for only in this way will he ever understand exactly what the person is trying to convey. This requires an openness of mind, an absence of prejudice or partiality, and a ready sympathy for the difficulties of the person, which are qualities which can only be cultivated by much inner searching and by practice and experience in helping others.

Communication takes place not only by words, but by such things as facial expression, posture and gestures, and the counsellor needs to be aware of and to understand the meaning of all these, and to be able to use them in connection with what he is told about the experiences of the person he is counselling. Things, such as flushing, excitability, dejection and bodily tensions supplement what is being said but sometimes they may belie the picture that is given by the person's words. Nor can the counsellor always be sure that his observation of an individual is accurate, and so while he makes a mental note, he needs to be ready to alter his first impressions by subsequent attitudes revealed

F

in conversation. Success in counselling is often completely obstructed by allowing first impressions to remain and colour all future observations. Furthermore people do not always behave at an interview in a manner which expresses their reason for coming, for the urgency of the occasion may raise attitudes from the unconscious which have been buried for a long time, and may seem completely foreign even to the person himself. These attitudes can be of great use to the counsellor provided he knows how to interpret them, and does not take them at their face value. Thus the blustering, awkward person may really be covering up his fear, shame of what he has come to discuss, or desire for understanding which he has thus far failed to receive from anyone.

Though it is advisable to follow some plan in every interview, which has either been thought out beforehand, when it is one of a series of interviews, or been decided upon after summing up what the person has come for at a single interview, much more will be learnt about the person if the interview in the first place is allowed to take an unstructured form. This should make the person feel that he is supplying information which he chooses to give, rather than being probed for relevant facts.

The first step in an interview is to help the person to relax and feel reasonably comfortable, and this may usually be done by encouraging him to state his purpose in coming and listening carefully while he speaks about what is at the top of his mind. Though this may not be entirely relevant, it does give the counsellor a chance to become acquainted with him, to learn something about his mode of expression, to suggest the kinds of comments, suggestions and questions which might later be asked and to give him some ideas as to the ways in which they should be framed. In this way the counsellor may more easily discern the point which the individual has reached, and so be more able to meet him at this point.

If the person talks first it will also tend to counteract any preconceived ideas about him which the counsellor may have himself entertained, particularly if he already knows the person. The ideal situation is one in which the counsellor and the person are unknown to one another. But quite often a counsellor may have heard something from a third party, may already know the person and think he has summed him up, or the person may have rung him up or written to him and suggested what is wrong. In each of these cases it is very easy to make a mistake which can influence the whole course of future interviews. The counsellor has, therefore, to start as far as possible from 'scratch', and use what information he has to justify rather than to determine the line the interview should take.

In this initial talking, much depends upon the responses of the counsellor, for he needs to encourage the person to continue talking without asking him to do so. Slight encouragement may be given by a nod or even by an attitude of attention, but often it is necessary to summarise what is said both to help the person to continue and to keep him to the point. Thus, 'I see that you are finding meeting your colleagues difficult' helps to focus the matter, while slight encouragement can be given by such words as: 'This seems to be troubling you; would you like to tell me more about it?'

An essential part of any counselling interview is to be able to listen, and this is perhaps one of the greatest arts and the most difficult to learn. It is the way in which the counsellor listens and the atmosphere which he creates for the person in doing so, that really counts. But such listening is not merely passive, it is a very active part of the counselling process. The counsellor needs both the will and the ability to listen.

It is essential that the person should feel that he is the only thing that matters at the moment. Since the slightest form of disturbance is likely to alter the form which the words of the person being counselled will take, or even the material that he is expressing, the telephone should not be allowed to ring or anyone else to come into the room. He should feel that he has all the interest and attention of the counsellor, and this depends very much upon the counsellor's own thoughts. If he is worried about his own personal affairs, these should be forgotten for the time being. He must put out of his mind any thoughts about a previous interview which may strike him and, perhaps most difficult of all, he must not concentrate so hard on something that the person has just said that he loses all consciousness of what is being said next. All this calls for complete relaxation on the part of the counsellor, the acknowledgment that all that is being said is of importance, and the confidence that he will be able to sort out the important from the less important matters when he recalls the interview.

Listening is not complete passivity and the counsellor's interest has to be shown. The 'feed-back' is a most important process in the whole matter of interpersonal communication. Even in ordinary conversation we usually look at the person we are talking to and depend very much on his smile, his obvious attention and his 'yes'. The counsellor often says 'mm' to indicate that he understands what has just been said without committing himself to the 'yes' which may imply agreement. Very much will depend upon his intonation and whether he can say 'mm' in a way which conveys both interest and sympathy.

Although the person should be encouraged to express his feelings, there is a danger in allowing them unlimited expression. Such feelings may be due not so much to a recent upsetting experience, as to a long chain of experiences going back into the remote past. These early experiences may have become twisted and distorted and interrelated with other things through the years, so that talking about them does not necessarily help the person or the counsellor, but opens up areas of the unconscious with which both are unequipped to deal. This can be an indication that more highly skilled treatment is required, and the counsellor needs to be aware of this at the earliest possible stage and to direct the person accordingly.

A disturbing situation, especially to the less experienced counsellor, is when the person remains silent, and this is often an occasion when the counsellor, usually mistakenly, tries to come in and fill the gap. The person may remain silent because he does not know how to verbalise his problem, and then the counsellor may have to help him. On the other hand he may be using silence to digest something that has been said. The counsellor needs to remember that he is probably far quicker at doing this than the person he is helping, and that when something entirely new is being realised it does take time to assimilate. The counsellor does well to remain silent too, lest he obstruct some valuable step forward. Silences are by no means easy to keep for the instinctive reaction is to break them. But the counsellor has to learn to keep silence when this is needed. At the same time he should continue to concentrate on what has just been said, for a change in the atmosphere of the silence can have just as disturbing an effect as breaking it.

Quite often the strangeness and emotion of the occasion may cause the person to pour out his troubles in the most entangled and unsystematic form, and the counsellor will be able to make little headway in discovering what is wrong. But again, listening rather than talking should be his reaction. If he interrupts such an outpouring because he wishes to clarify some point, or because he suddenly thinks of a question which he feels he should ask, he may stem the whole flow and lose the most valuable points. Or worse still, he may lose the confidence of the person, who feels that after all he was mistaken in thinking that the counsellor would understand.

This does not mean that the counsellor never asks a question. It is often necessary to do so. But the content of the question and the point at which it is asked must be linked with what the person is expressing, rather than when the counsellor thinks of it. To ask a person to reveal confidences before his own confidence is won is to court defeat. In general, leading rather than pointed questions should be asked, and questions that cannot be answered by a brief 'yes' or 'no'. Such questions stimulate the person to talk more freely and avoid the always present danger of putting answers into his mouth. By rephrasing some of the words which the person has spoken in question form and reslanting the emphasis, it is often possible to ask something without giving the feeling that the person is being categorised. Thus, 'You did take her to hospital, didn't you?' both emphasises the need for some medical attention and enquires what was done in the particular situation.

Another use of questioning is to encourage the person to talk in relevant areas where he finds the going difficult, and remarks such as 'I don't understand, could you explain it to me more fully?' help him to elaborate the matter in more detail, and also gives him the encouragement to continue as he feels that he is not only concentrating upon himself but is also being of some use to the counsellor.

There are no specific questions that can be used on certain defined occasions, and it is usually a mistake to frame the same question in a similar way to every person who comes. The only exception is perhaps the name and address of the person, which will normally be required for the purpose of records. This too may come up in the course of conversation and so need not specifically be asked. Nor should it always be asked at the same stage. It can come as well at the end of an interview as at the beginning, and is often more suitably asked when the person feels more at home and able to give information without feeling that it is being dragged from him.

It is often the manner and tone of voice in which the question is asked, rather than the content of the question which is of importance. If the counsellor gives the impression that he is prying into somebody else's business, he will usually make very little headway. Or if he seems to be taking an undue interest in facts which are perhaps unsalubrious he may get elaboration which is far from the truth. His manner needs to be such as to convey the encouragement of friendliness without the intimacy of the more ordinary type of friendship.

Closely allied to questioning are the comments of the counsellor. Sometimes the only difference lies in the inflection of the speaker's voice. 'You find life at home pretty difficult' can either be a query or a comment, depending upon whether the pitch of the voice is raised or lowered on the last syllables. In general the counsellor should comment only for purposes similar to those for which he asks the question – either to reassure or to encourage the person, and so to lead him on to discuss further relevant matters.

There are, perhaps, three kinds of intervention into which the inexperienced counsellor is likely to fall. He may be encouraged to relate his own personal experience because it seems to correspond with that of the person he is counselling. But similarity of experience creates no tie between two separate lives. In the most favourable cases, the person will show some understanding, and may listen and become himself the counsellor. At the other extreme he may become keenly resentful and cruelly disappointed and refuse to continue the interview. If the counsellor does feel that he should mention some experience of his own, it must have some relevance to the reason for which the person has come to see him, and also fulfil some useful purpose in connection with this.

A second kind of inexperienced intervention is the giving of a personal opinion. Some counsellors would say that this should never be done, although others would permit it, provided the time was carefully chosen. An opinion offered at the wrong moment or with insufficient time for the person to express himself may result in the person deciding that he is not understood and perhaps feeling that nobody will ever understand him, and so he might as well cease seeking help.

A third thing which is very easy to do is to minimise the

experience of the person, and to try to encourage him by suggesting that 'it was not really as bad as all that', or that 'if you try to forget about it, it will be all right'. The counsellor is then looking at the matter in a theoretical way, and although his judgement may be objective, the problem is isolated from its content. It is detached from the actual experience which gave rise to it and conferred on it its true meaning. Thus, once again, the person will feel misunderstood and disinclined to pursue the matter further.

Counsellors are sometimes asked personal questions which they may not know how to answer or even whether they should answer them. Usually such questions are asked either because the person thinks it is polite or the social thing to do, or because the relationship between the person and the counsellor is becoming closer. In the former case the person is not usually particularly interested in the answer. He does not really care whether the counsellor is married or whether he plays football, and if the discussion is directed back to his own problems he will be glad to continue with what is to him a much more absorbing matter. In the latter case the person may be trying to find out whether the counsellor is the sort of person he had envisaged, and whether he can be trusted. Then a frank, brief and truthful answer is what is usually desirable, with a quick re-direction of the conversation back to the person's own problems. Sometimes, of course, such a question may indicate the hidden desire or concern of the person himself, and the recognition of this may be of profound use to the counsellor. It is therefore rarely wise to rebuff a person's question, however embarrassing it may be, but to give a brief, and perhaps impersonal answer.

Since practical difficulties may be at the root of many troubles the counsellor needs to bear these in mind when talking to a person. Such things as sickness or a handicap, difficult relationships at home, or at work, alcoholism, instability of character and a period of mental illness, may come to light through the form that the conversation takes at the interview.

Sometimes such difficulties may be recalled through the association of ideas. When a person is talking about some subject, he may make what seems to the counsellor to be a quite irrelevant remark about some entirely different situation. A man may be talking about his difficulties with his wife, and then suddenly switch over to his mother whom he idolised. This could indicate that his own problem is not isolated, but closely connected with an earlier situation. Unexpected and inexplicable associations are often the key to basic difficulties.

Shifts in conversation are somewhat similar for they may be a continuation, in the unconscious part of the person, of some particular difficulty. More often, however, they may occur because the person feels that he is telling too much and does not want to reveal himself further. Or they may happen when a person is beginning to talk about material of a deep personal nature or of something which is too condemning of the character which the person wishes to present or which is very painful for him to pursue. They could also be an indication that the counsellor is not giving his full attention or understanding.

The first words which a person says when an interview starts and the manner in which he states his problem are often of unusual significance. These can have various meanings according to the personality and the circumstances in which they occur, but they are rarely without some purport. Similarly the concluding remarks at the end of an interview are worth attention for a person will often sum up what he has got out of the interview or the degree to which his forces have been mobilised for going ahead and working out his problem.

A person's story is rarely unified, and he often contradicts himself or conceals his meaning. Such behaviour may indicate the operation of some internal pressure such as guilt, confusion or anxiety. A person may be truthful in some statements, but untruthful in others. He may tell a straightforward story, but with unexpected gaps in which it is impossible to elicit information. Frequently these areas are of particular importance, and may suggest some significant factor. On the other hand they may be chance mental aberrations. The counsellor of small experience will often attach too much importance to them though when they occur several times they are usually worthy of note. Discrimination is needed in deciding whether such things are significant, but on the other hand they should not be ignored.

Recurrent references can be another sign of deeper trouble. Sometimes a person will continually return to a certain subject, such as his job or difficulties with his wife, which may indicate some lack of balance. Or he may talk freely enough, but not manage to move forward. He may complain about something to which the counsellor has a satisfactory answer, but which the person seems unable to realise. There may be some reason why he sticks at this point, particularly if a question as to what he thinks he could do about it, fails to make him move on.

Although the purpose of counselling is to help a person to understand himself more fully, and so be able to readjust his life to meet the situation in which he is involved, it is nearly always necessary for the person to make some change in himself as well. The process by which he does this is called 'insight', and it emerges gradually from within the personality, as the person discovers new emotional strength and develops a greater recreativeness towards his life. It usually involves an acceptance of the impulses and urges which may have led up to the situation; an understanding of the experiences which have brought reactions such as fear, guilt or hate; and the capacity to look at one's own conflicts impartially and to choose possible ways of dealing with them. Real insight, therefore, results in facing difficulties and conflicts honestly, working through them, and finding the capacity to express positive rather than negative tendencies, with initiative and spontaneity.

Usually such insight develops within the counselling relationship by stages. First of all there will be an awareness that something is wrong, that a problem exists, and that help is needed. Then, when help is sought, there will come some understanding of the issues involved, particularly those which have some bearing upon human relationships. This will be followed by the realisation on the part of the person that perhaps part of the cause lies within himself. He needs therefore to understand his own feelings and motives, particularly the nature of his instinctive drives, the deeper cause of his anxieties, and his underlying feelings of hatred and guilt. He also must discover the various defences that he has put up against these. In this way he can begin to understand himself.

It is the counsellor's task to help the person to bring into the open those thoughts, attitudes and feelings which are emotionally charged and which centre around the problems and conflicts he has come to tell about. It is the unrecognised emotional factors which are usually basic, and to bring these to the surface and to get the person to recognise them is one of the most difficult skills to acquire. The counsellor has to develop the ability to pay attention to the feeling tone of what is being said as well as to its superficial content and to bring feelings consciously into the picture without taking sides. But he is not expected to arouse these feelings and emotions. This is the function of the psychotherapist and it is very dangerous for the counsellor to meddle with them.

Nevertheless, feelings may be directed not only towards others, but also to the counsellor himself in the form of transference. Feelings which may be projected in this way are feelings of love or hate, of fear or anger, of hope or desire, and it may be a valuable experience for the person to form for a time a relationship in which such feelings towards somebody can be simply and naturally expressed without fear of rebuttal. But the counsellor needs to be aware that this may happen, and be ready to recognise his own reaction or counter-transference. Quite often it is only the counsellor who is aware of the transference taking place. The person himself may merely feel excessively disgruntled or pleased with the counsellor at some stage in the counselling.

Such feelings are often emotions which were not expressed at the time because of the fears attached to them. Therefore they may appear at first in disguise, such as scepticism about the usefulness of the counselling, failure to arrive on time, or exemplary good manners which obviously hide what the person really feels. The counsellor can only bring these feelings to the surface by allowing them to be exercised upon himself. Then, when they are consciously acknowledged their source can be gradually appreciated, and they can be recognised for what they are. Once this happens, the relationship between counsellor and person being counselled will be able to resume its usual form.

Since insight involves the perception of self and of the nature of certain attitudes and impulses which have been disturbing, the uninhibited expression of feeling has great value in this respect, for in this way a person can gain emotional release from those feelings and attitudes which he has been repressing. He reaches a greater understanding of himself as he talks freely about his feelings, and he becomes able to face the various aspects of his personality without rationalising or denial. He is better able to take a frank look at himself, and make a true evaluation of what he is and why he has been behaving in a particular way.

When such an interpretation of the situation is being worked out by the person and the counsellor together, the counsellor should not give the impression that he has deeper knowledge and understanding than the person has, or wants him to have at any particular moment. He can neither go ahead nor behind, but must respond to the level of feeling that the person is expressing, even though he may already have a very clear idea as to what changes should be made. Only in this way will the person begin to get some insight into his situation.

This is where some knowledge of psychology and of psychological types on the part of the counsellor is useful, for it gives him a lead as to what to expect, and also some idea as to when to try to help the person to reach a more mature outlook on life. The counsellor has not only to help the person to become aware of some of the emotional factors which have brought the problem into being and which without such knowledge makes the problem appear insoluble. He may also have to use his wisdom and discretion in communicating his interpretation to the person. In doing this he needs to wait until it seems that the thought or idea which may be helpful is near the surface of the person's mind. In order to help him to receive it the counsellor must be in close emotional alignment with the person. He must be also able to convey it in a way likely to be convincing, that is in simple language which is easily understood and in a manner which will make the person feel he has a full share in making the discovery. Insight and understanding are most effective, of course, when they arise spontaneously, but the counsellor may need to further the process by clarifying new understandings and helping the person to formulate the meaning of the insight which he has achieved.

Insight often consists in enabling the person to reach a more satisfactory association with the past, the future or some particular external circumstances. In some people, past experiences leave a vague but unquestionable feeling of uneasiness. Others give up or feel that the past rules out the possible success of any new undertaking, They accept their defeat and no longer even try. In direct contrast are those who rebel at the sight of their past failure. They want to prove, no matter what the price, that they can succeed. So they make the same attempt, over and over again using very similar methods. Insight means that they begin to accept the past as a given fact, and build on from there.

Others find all their decisions of no use because of the uncertainty of the future. They accept the past for what it is, but they cannot do the same about the future. They have not the courage to face their present responsibilities, and so they desire the future to be fixed once and for all. Such persons can only rid themselves of this utopian desire by learning to accept the future as a gradual development and one which they will be able to meet when it comes.

Another person may find some external circumstance insurmountable. It gradually becomes an obsession to him and seems inescapable. He feels so frightened and unprotected that he tries to elude all the tensions that are involved and to avoid all the efforts that are demanded of him. When he discovers that flight is unrealisable, he gradually recedes into an imaginary world. He too has to accept these circumstances before he can begin to cope with them.

Once a person begins to accept the past, the future and any other circumstances for what they are in reality, radical changes take place. They become not 'the' but 'his' past and future and circumstances of 'his' life. Since they are more intimately related to him, he can more easily cope with them. A consciousness of this encourages him to investigate the real state of affairs and to examine without fear all the elements of his experience. What he had tried to do, without success, he can now attack from other angles, and although he may not succeed at once, he will learn something at each attempt. This may involve a choice of more satisfying goals which only now appear desirable, or of forming some new relationship which only now is possible.

When the problem is small or when the person is quickly able to understand its meaning then, once insight is gained, a solution may be found. But with most problems it is a matter of gaining a little insight, of understanding the problem a little better and repeating these processes until a more complete understanding is secured. This will often take quite a long time and may never be fully achieved. In fact sometimes problems are beyond the reach both of the person being counselled, and of the counsellor himself, and this has to be faced frankly. It usually happens when there are deep-seated emotional difficulties, or firmly fixed character disorders. It is then necessary to encourage the person to go to a trained consultant or psychotherapist.

The final stage in counselling is, therefore, to reach some sort of solution to the problem, and this should come quite naturally as the person grows in a knowledge of himself and his potentialities. By this time the person will be under far less strain and anxiety, and will be working in much closer co-operation with the counsellor. He will be less on the defensive and more able to accept himself fully. This is the chance for the counsellor to introduce some re-educative ideas, not so much in the form of a solution to the problem, but as a way of meeting the situation in a more constructive manner. Sometimes at this stage some definite decision has to be made and therefore there will be a need to go into the advantages and disadvantages of different lines of action with the counsellor. Even then the choice must remain that of the person, and will not necessarily be that which the counsellor would advocate.

When the person is able to cope with the situation himself in his own way, it is time for the counselling to cease, for the person should now be able to use what he has learnt, not only for this particular situation, but also for others as well. In fact, he should have become more mature and so be able to deal more satisfactorily with the problems of life. The ending of a series of interviews is not always easy, for the person will often have ambivalent views about it. He may at one moment feel quite capable of carrying on, on his own, and at another still feel the need of some support. There will also have developed a close and understanding relationship between the counsellor and the person he is helping which will tend to bind them together. The conclusion of counselling should be just as significant, clear-cut and helpful as any other part of the therapeutic contact. It is therefore important that the counsellor should be alert to the person's progress and that as soon as independence is evident he should bring up the possibility of ending the contacts. In this way a break will be anticipated and when it is made will not come as a shock. If the person has selected appropriate goals and has the courage and confidence to work towards them he is likely to proceed more quickly after the conclusion of counselling.

Counselling does not always proceed at this pace, nor in this logical and clear-cut manner, for there is no limit to the types of people who may come to the counsellor nor to the variety of human problems which they may bring. Sometimes a person comes to an interview, not with a deep-seated problem, but with the desire to think aloud and the need for some sympathetic and impartial interest. In this case the counsellor will have to be the expert listener, and be able to provide that amount of support which will enable the person to go away refreshed and re-assured and so better able to assess the importance of his difficulties and the way of dealing with them.

In many instances the person will have thought through the problem logically himself, be able to advance arguments which are solid and be capable of reaching a wise and realistic line of action with little delay. The counsellor may only be called upon to clarify some points or fill in some omissions which have been made. It will be quite apparent that once the person is convinced that this is the right line of action to take he is capable of following it.

More often, however, the problem will not be brought with clarity, order, balance or calm assurance. There may be a sketchy outline of a few words or a confused narrative with side-tracking at every detail. The person may describe the situation quite well, but reach no conclusion or what he says may be devoid of any positive value. He obviously wishes to unload his responsibility on to the counsellor, and sooner or later will ask, 'What must I do?' It is only as he talks and becomes aware of what is possible for him that any progress can be made.

Few people are able at once to accept the fact that their condition may depend on factors outside their control – such things as temperament, character, education, social milieu – and that they must do the best that they can under the circumstances. More usually there is a long and weary struggle of disappointments and successes as a person learns to accept his difficulties as enriching experiences which help him to come to know himself. The rhythm of such interviews is necessarily slow and the counsellor will need much patience in encouraging the person without pressing him. A final solution may never be reached, but the person may be better able to carry on and should be able to return periodically when things become particularly difficult.

Sometimes a person will deliberately call a halt himself, because a critical point has been reached, and he prefers not to delve too deeply. The counsellor must again respect the will of the person and create circumstances which make it possible for him to return in the future if he wants. A somewhat similar situation arises when the person has been sent unwillingly to the counsellor by his parents, some interested relative or friend, or by a doctor or minister. He does not wish to talk, and dialogue can only develop if both parties desire it. The counsellor has the difficult task of securing his co-operation and of reaching a relationship of complete freedom and equality with him. This may mean suggesting another interview when the person feels inclined, for it is essential that such a relationship should be reached before the process of counselling begins.

The counsellor will also meet those people whose immaturity of outlook and personal habits suggest that they have never acquired normal social and ethical standards of behaviour. A change will sometimes come about by slowly building up a relationship with them through offers of warm friendship and understanding, such as might be provided by a wise and kindly parent. But there will be many disappointments and very little progress. The chaos and disorder in which such people live has to be viewed with a great measure of detachment if they are not to feel that they are being censured or blamed. Their early experiences have given them little opportunity of developing those aspects of personality or character which might have made them able to meet the responsibilities of life in a more mature manner. Counselling cannot change this, though sometimes it is possible to strengthen a weak character and foster some emotional growth. The most that the counsellor can do is to give them support and be available to them as often as possible.

On occasions a person who comes for counselling may never reach the stage of showing any constructive insight. He may talk about his difficulties continuously, or about someone else's difficulties, without managing to reveal anything of his inner self. He may lose his way in a flood of empty words or superficial observations. Or he may choose a line of action without any conviction or with premature enthusiasm. Such resistance is usually due to some psychological disturbance. The person perceives, at least confusedly, that he needs help, yet he cannot resolve to look for that help where it can be found. He knows that his reactions are not proportionate to the factors that stimulate them, that they are out of place or morbid, but he does not know what to do about it. The fact that he is conscious of this indicates his neurotic attitude, and distinguishes his state from both a superficial disturbance and from a clearly defined mental illness. This consciousness is the best criterion to the counsellor who has not been trained in depth psychology or in psychiatry. But all he can do is to inform the person of possible forms of treatment and where he might be able to receive it.

There are people who are unable to grasp or perceive their incapacity. They may bury themselves in a dream world or be so accustomed to the strange way in which they live that they do not react against their isolation. They will rarely come to a counsellor spontaneously, and if they are sent will either have nothing to say or enter upon a tirade against the counsellor or those who have sent them. No dialogue is possible for they have alienated themselves from their problem. It then becomes the duty of the counsellor to assume responsibility for them, by firmly referring them to a medical specialist. If there is something organically wrong this is fairly easy, but otherwise it may become necessary to contact a member of the family or an employer. In doing this the counsellor is necessarily abandoning his role of counselling and assuming that of direction.

Failure may occur, of course, through the inexperience or the bungling of the counsellor, and then there needs to be a frank recognition of the fact, and an agreement to cease interviews. This may lead to a clarification of the barriers, and so to new therapeutic developments. If it does not, it at least prevents defensive action on both sides and stops the growth of feelings of guilt or recrimination. The person will feel that at least the counsellor is honest, and will not be put off using the process of counselling again.

Like any form of therapy, counselling has its practical problems. First of all there is the length of interview and the spacing between interviews. It is generally accepted that concentration of the sort required in counselling is difficult and so it is usual to fix interviews of an hour or an hour and a half in length. It is often advisable to tell the person this at the beginning of an interview so that he is prepared for it and does not feel that he is being cut off in the middle of a conversation. If he saves up important things for the end of an interview, this is often the opportunity for fixing another.

The spacing of interviews should depend very much on the desire of the person concerned. When things are difficult he may like to come frequently but later he may feel that a greater length of time should elapse between interviews. It is usually unwise to fix interviews at less than a week apart, for the person needs that length of time to assimilate any new insights or gains in knowledge and to make some sort of assessment of his progress. Broken appointments are likely to occur and, as we have seen, are often the sign that a certain stage has been reached in the treatment. When the time has come for something paritcularly distasteful to be discussed there may be a conscious or unconscious desire to break appointments or to cease coming altogether. The counsellor needs to make it as easy as possible for the person to return, or not to return if he prefers.

On the question of note-taking, most counsellors agree that this is not desirable during interviews. On the whole it is better to set aside a few minutes directly after an interview to jot down a few notes with regard to what has occurred rather than to give a more formal atmosphere to the interview by note-taking. Since it is emotional attitudes as much as facts that are important, it is these which should be recorded in detail, and in a way that makes it possible to obtain at a glance the stage which has been reached as a setting for the next interview. It is usually unnecessary to look back further than the previous interview when preparing to receive a person.

When notes are taken, the matter of confidentiality arises to a greater extent than with the spoken word. It is usual not to divulge anything that has been said at an interview without the permission of the person concerned. With written notes this is more difficult, for someone may inadvertently read them. It is often useful to adopt a form of shorthand of one's own, or to omit names in records which may be seen by other people. A further difficulty is what to tell relatives, especially in close relationships such as husband and wife. A non-committal but encouraging statement is the form that is often used, and one which usually meets the case unless there is an obvious need to inform a close relative on some matter.

Circumstances may make it necessary for counselling to be brief. This may happen when the problem is immediate as in the case of bereavement or desertion. The person will then need support at the moment and clarification later on. But quite often it is impossible to see the person more than once or twice, as, for example, when a person is in hospital for only a few days. It should not alter the pattern which the counsellor follows, but it may mean that less time can be taken in getting to the root of the problem, and so the person cannot be left entirely to make his own pace. On the other hand it may not be thought desirable to do more than give some shape and design to the feelings and thoughts of the person as he expresses them. Sometimes this will make it possible for the person to deal with the problem himself. Or he may discover that counselling has something to offer to his state of mind, and so may seek further help. It is always useful to suggest someone to whom he might go, though not usually wise to make any arrangements for him to do so unless specifically asked. A person will often have his own ideas as to the sort of person in whom he feels able to confide.

The experienced counsellor will always have the threefold pattern of problem relating, insight and solution clearly within his mind and he will inevitably follow this sequence. But the amount of time he spends on each stage, the extent they overlap, and the number of times he will have to return to an earlier stage are infinite. His success will depend to a very large extent upon his understanding of personality, his familiarity with the techniques of counselling and his ability to apply them with finesse and wisdom. It will also depend upon his own personality, for before a person can be counselled he has to come to the counsellor, and a person will only talk intimately to another person if he feels that he will really be understood.

VI. The Pastoral Counsellor

Since counselling involves a process of relationship between the person coming for help and the one who gives it, much of its success depends upon the personality and training of the counsellor. Our response to another person is affected both by our own emotional make-up, and by the kind of role which is regarded as being proper to the job we happen to be doing. A successful counsellor has to be aware both of his own emotional make-up and of the kind of impression which he makes upon others, and he has to see that these do not encroach upon the relationship with the person he is counselling. Training will help him with this, but no amount of training will compensate for a personality which is immature or insecure.

People differ greatly in their response to others. Some respond with kindness and helpfulness to signs of weakness; others are apt to be rather impatient with them, and much more tolerant of the angry, blustering type of person. Different types of difficulties affect people who are listening to them in very different ways. Some are critical of financial disorders but tolerant of sexual aberrations, or tolerant of cruelty to adults but not to children. Others condemn inefficiency at work, but are quite unmoved by incompetence in household affairs. A counsellor has to discover where his biases and prejudices lie, and so be able to keep his feelings in perspective. He has to be aware of his instinctive reactions to a highly emotional person or situation, and be able to control them so that he can make an entirely neutral approach. This is not easy to achieve for a person rarely knows exactly how he responds to or appears to other people.

Similarly there is the tendency to assume a certain role, such as that of a parent, a teacher, a business executive or a clergyman, which is carried over into our other relationships. This role is bound to have some effect upon our response to another person, even if it is not apparent in our appearance. It may tend to inhibit the other person from feeling entirely free to talk, and it will certainly have some effect upon the counsellor's attitude, for he will feel obliged to uphold his role and to make the appropriate sort of response. This is one of the major difficulties involved in pastoral counselling, whether it is undertaken by an ordained minister of a church, or by a Christian who feels that his beliefs cannot be entirely omitted from the counselling process.

If a counsellor is an ordained minister, his role in the eyes of the person who comes for counselling is one of the initial difficulties which has to be overcome. In the United States, where people frequently turn to the pastor for counselling, he is often consulted as a psychologist. This has its disadvantages, for few pastors are fully trained for this work and those who are find it difficult to fit this work in with their other pastoral duties. On the other hand, it does at least help a person to seek counselling with a Christian minister if he feels that moral issues may not be weighted nor religious matters over-emphasised. People rarely turn to the clergy in England because on the whole the image of the clergyman is not that of the understanding pastor, and they think that they will only get spiritual help, which is not usually what they feel they need. This is only likely to change when any preconceived ideas as to the role which the clergyman is likely to follow in counselling is forgotten, and when it is felt that there is complete freedom for both the counsellor and the person who comes to him for help to work through the problems together.

Nevertheless, pastoral counselling does differ from ordinary counselling in that the aim of pastoral counselling is not only to help a person to improve his relationships with other people and to understand himself, but also to reach a more realistic approach to the divine relationship. God can rarely be entirely omitted from pastoral counselling and ethical and religious matters are very likely to arise. This will not alter the principles or the techniques used, but it may have some effect upon the direction which the counselling will take.

The method of counselling which has been described so far is often known as 'non-directive' counselling. It assumes that the healthy outcome of counselling depends upon the freedom of the person to express his will in defining his goals and in solving his problems, and also in establishing a meaningful relationship between himself and the counsellor which may be the pattern for other relationships between himself and his fellow men. Some pastoral counsellors feel that their special position within a church necessitates a more directive and authoritarian approach than is indicated here.

It is for this reason that some pastoral counsellors employ what is called 'directive' counselling. In this type of counselling the counsellor studies the problem which the person brings to him by asking leading questions. He accumulates a sheaf of evidence by which he hopes to make a diagnosis and to interpret what may be hidden to the person. He adopts the authoritarian role that he knows what is best for the person before him, and he proceeds to choose the goals which the person has been unable to choose for himself, and to advise him how best to move towards them. If the person resists, he will produce the reasons why he has chosen these goals, and either press him to change his mind or offer him an alternative solution.

A person who comes to such a counsellor will come on the understanding that, provided the counsellor judges correctly, the answer to his problem will gradually be revealed to him. It is the method which has been followed by spiritual advisers for a very long time, and provided there is no underlying psychological condition which the counsellor does not understand, and that the person is willing to be guided by someone whom he thinks is far better equipped to solve his problems than he is himself, little harm is likely to be done. This was the method which was used by spiritual directors like St Ignatius of Loyola, St John of the Cross, and St Francis of Sales, and their success lay in their deep understanding of human nature which combined a knowledge both of the underlying as well as the apparent cause of the problems which were brought to them.

But indiscriminate directive counselling can cause the person to take less and less responsibility himself. He sees the counsellor playing the dominant role, and so he himself becomes submissive and passively assents. The counsellor to him represents the father figure with the result that he feels dependent and regresses to childish immaturity. On the other hand, he may strike out for independence by an adolescent revolt against the authority wielded over him. He may resist what the counsellor is trying to put over to him, and either refuse to acquiesce or lose interest in the whole affair and so fail to come for further interviews. Then the effect of this counselling upon him may not only be time wasted, but it could be harmful.

Although a clear distinction has been made between directive and non-directive counselling, in actual fact the counsellor is never in an entirely passive role. He must be alert every minute to see the deeper meanings, to sense the direction of the person's gropings, and to follow the clues skilfully, and in these ways he is indirectly guiding the progress which the person is making. Without giving advice, he affirms insights, clarifies issues, states alternatives, and encourages positive steps of action when these are chosen by the person. The extent to which he does this depends upon the state of mind of the person who comes to him for help.

In order to reach a middle way between these two approaches, some counsellors follow what is called the 'eclectic method', which adapts itself to the demands of the situation and allows the counsellor freedom to use one or other of these methods as seems fitting, or to blend the two together. Each individual has ultimately to assume responsibility for his own life, but many people who come to a counsellor are neither ready to assume such responsibility nor able alone to solve their problems through sympathetic and understanding counsel. The counsellor has then to assume some initiative and provide some suggestions. But he remains open-minded as he helps the person to explore his problems and to adapt himself to his world. Thus the method is adaptive rather than dogmatic. The aim is still to help the person help himself, and if he is emotionally upset he is encouraged to express his feelings and emotions. But if he is in need of information and advice, and is emotionally as well as intellectually ready to receive it, he is provided with it.

Many people who come to a counsellor are basically able to solve their own problems, but are baffled by some special circumstances which have occurred. Then this eclectic approach may help. The person and the counsellor are joint investigators and evaluators. Both contribute their points of view to the solution of the problem, although ultimately the person chooses the action he will take. In the process of discussion the counsellor decides the degree of responsibility which he is going to assume and arranges his responses in such a way that the person is not being indoctrinated or imposed upon. He enriches the person's discussions and actions without dominating them and the relationship is based on the mutuality of friendship and fellowship. The counsellor supplies a sense of security, with an objective recognition of the person's own gifts and skills and his capacity to participate in making a decision. In this atmosphere, which is sometimes called 'nurture', the person is enabled to look more objectively at his difficulties and is encouraged to face them himself without feeling coerced or driven.

Sometimes it is the type of problem, rather than the sort of person or the special circumstances, which determines the method used by the counsellor. Some problems are obviously straightforward and concerned directly with the spiritual life. A person who has recently become a Christian may need guidance about matters of personal faith or about formulations of doctrine, about the assurance of salvation or personal consecration. Others may be concerned about the meaning of life or worried about death and the hereafter. Primary religious matters such as these cannot be dealt with by the methods of non-directive counselling. The counsellor has his fundamental beliefs which he is bound to convey in these circumstances, and it is often wise to point this out when it is realised that a person has come with this sort of problem.

But more often problems are of a secondary religious nature, such as the obligation of a Christian to the community or to his family or of conduct evoked by the nature of his work. A very large group of problems which are brought to a counsellor are personal ones of a practical kind occasioned by the conditions of everyday living. The counsellor is then the sympathetic, supporting friend, sharing burdens gladly, but not necessarily discussing deeper spiritual matters unless specifically asked. Many apparent religious problems have deep emotional roots. Then counselling skills have to come into play, for such problems are usually a guise behind which more intimate and important dilemmas lurk.

Some problems are problems of conscience, for no person is without conflicts and tensions about feelings, values, aims and ideals, and these conflicts are unusually strong and mixed. The Christian concept of conflict is the discrepancy between the way man was meant to be, and the way he actually is. Since man was created by God in his own image, inherent in this image is the freedom to make moral choices. But when man uses this freedom to choose evil, his choice corrupts his inner purity, and the evil, which was previously external to him, becomes a part of him. Remnants of the image, however, remain and a terrific tension develops between these two opposites of good and evil in the character of man. This tension becomes increasingly unbearable as man continues to make moral decisions which are evil rather than good, and so he tries to find a way out of this morass. Quite often the search is for an escape instead of a solution, and in running away from his problem, a person not only postpones coming to grips with it, but because his way of escape is away from reality it creates a problem in itself. This is the moral situation with which the pastoral counsellor is frequently faced, and it is in terms of this situation that he has to provide guidance.

It is through man's conscience that he recognises this conflict between good and evil, or what he would call right and wrong. A sense of guilt pervades his outlook, and the only way in which the tension in the human conscience can be reduced is to remove this sense of guilt. When this happens, the destructive emotions that caused the vicious cycle of personality disintegration lose their force, and the person is freed to become his true self. So far as the Christian is concerned, there are no inner resources for wholeness within man until he is at peace with himself and his God over the basic conflict between the way he is and the way he was meant to be.

Most forms of religion have fostered a sense of guilt as a necessary spiritual discipline, leading to repentance and forgiveness and so to the wholeness of man and his acceptance by God. But psychology looks at conscience and guilt in a somewhat different way and shows that guilty attitudes and feelings are not always what they appear to be. In Freud's terminology the super-ego is the conscience, which the child develops as he is forced by the attitudes of parents, teachers and playmates to control those primitive impulses and emotional wants in the interests of the outside environment. He gradually takes into himself the demands, ideas, standards and values of his parents and other important adults and there arises within him a super-ego whose main function is to make him follow the parental line. Fear always plays a large part in this, because it enforces the child's subordination to standards of feeling and action which are not his own. This may lead to resentment and pent-up aggressiveness, and so a sense of guilt develops whenever parental and other adult claims are not met. If smothered resentment and aggression grow and are further repressed by fear and guilt, a hidden vicious circle can arise. Some of this regression may seep out as irritability and crises of temper, but much of it may be turned back inwards and become the basis for a ruthlessly repressive persecuting conscience in a guilt-laden mind.

The true moral conscience, however, is very different from this. It grows alongside, or is intermingled with the super-ego and the task of moral growth is the replacement of the super-ego by a mature adult conscience. Gradually the realisation comes that values are not just the result of private and individual whim, but that there exists a system of values that is objective and not necessarily the same as the particular code of conduct or custom which society accepts. It is a system of values which the universal experience of mankind has found to be good in living in personal relationship. The question as to whether such values are self-evidencing, or are in themselves a manifestation of the ultimate spiritual reality of God is where the psychologist parts company with the Christian.

The development of a true moral conscience takes place slowly, as the capacity to reflect upon the distinctions which others make between good and evil increases. Then a personal moral insight becomes progressively possible. The super-ego weakens as the adult conscience develops and an independent ethical judgement, with a willingness to learn from others, gradually takes its place. Relatively few people, however, develop fully a true moral conscience. Most have a conscience which is a curious mixture of super-ego and independent moral judgement, and some do not mature beyond the stage of the child.

Feelings of guilt are constantly brought to the pastoral counsellor and they usually contain, as well as any real moral issue, a very large element of fear of punishment, going back to the days of parental control. The stronger this sort of guilt grows, the more it weakens the capacity for constructive effort and diverts the mind away in a morbid self-recrimination from genuine change and moral improvement. Thus guilty feelings have to be very carefully assessed as to whether they have any real moral or religious significance. They are very different from ethical condemnation or healthy self-criticism of a courageously objective kind which is combined with a determination to bring about changes in character. Father Grou indicates the difference in this passage from his *Manual for Interior Souls*:

> The truly devout man does not perplex himself; he goes on courageously; he is not over scrupulous. If he falls into a fault he does not agitate himself; he humbles himself at the sight of his weakness; he raises himself up and thinks no more about it. He is not astonished at his weakness, at his falls or his imperfections; he is never discouraged. . . . If he were to fall a hundred times a day he would not despair, but would stretch out his hands lovingly to God, and beg of Him to lift him up.[7]

Guilt feelings are usually the signs of moral sickness, while ethical condemnation points to sin. Religion has often failed to make this distinction, with disastrous results. Moral sickness has a compulsive character which springs from the unconscious and which usually has its origins in the repression of conflicts in the past. Its victim is quite unable to resist or control it, and is frequently unaware of its presence. Sin, on the other hand, is conscious and wilful and well within the control of the individual. It involves a rejection of accepted moral values, and means to the Christian a wilful breaking of his relationship with God.

The difficulty which the counsellor meets is that wrong-doing is often a combination of several factors. As we have seen, much of human behaviour is influenced by the past and often quite unconsciously. Environmental influences also play an important part, while the actual incident itself may be entirely accidental and the result of a fortuitous combination of circumstances. Thus it is impossible to speak of the magnitude of a particular misdemeanour without reference to the person who has committed it and the circumstances in which it took place. A counsellor cannot overlook sin when it is apparent, but it has to be seen against the background of its history and motivation and understood accordingly. The modern tendency to explain away all evil behaviour as symptoms of some deeper disturbance rather than sin is having its effects on the public conscience. It leads directly to a general diminution of the sense of personal responsibility, with very dangerous results. The pastoral counsellor has the difficult task of discovering the extent to which a person is responsible for what he does, and when this is deemed necessary of pointing out his misdemeanour to him.

This raises the question of the extent to which the Christian counsellor can really countenance the wrong-doing of the person he is helping. As we have seen, a basic principle of counselling is acceptance, and this acceptance extends to the whole man. It embraces all the concrete aspects in his present situation and his past life. It involves his social position, his intellectual capacities and his natural talents. The social failure is accepted in the same way as the socially successful. Even unacceptable acts, such as violations of the civil or moral law do not deprive the person of the acceptance or respect of the counsellor.

But approving is a very different matter. Perhaps one of the greatest difficulties of the counsellor is to resolve the confusion between acceptance and approval. The person comes for help because he is aware that there is something disturbing in his life and he does not feel happy about it. The counsellor's role is to help the person proceed from a situation which is undesirable and unacceptable to a situation which is both desirable and acceptable. In order to do this all the uncongenial qualities, feelings and attitudes need to be discussed in an accepting atmosphere, for otherwise they might not be revealed in their entirety.

But this does not mean that the counsellor necessarily approves of them. The Christian counsellor has a philosophy of life which includes convictions about moral right and wrong in human behaviour; but if these convictions are introduced at an inappropriate moment they are likely to be misunderstood or misinterpreted, and so to mar the whole counselling process. The counsellor has to accept without approval or disapproval every bit of information which he can discover about the person, and only at the appropriate moment disclose what he thinks is morally right.

No one but the counsellor can decide exactly when this moment comes. It depends upon the person himself and his gradual growth to maturity. As counselling proceeds and he begins to leave behind him some of his childhood attitudes and to replace them with a more adult approach his aims and values in life will change. This will happen almost imperceptibly but the sensitive counsellor will be able to judge just when it is possible to discuss the rights and wrongs of some erroneous attitude or form of behaviour. It is not usually his function to bring it up but to make it possible, perhaps by some leading question, for the person to do so. Then, as the person discovers for himself that his conduct is questionable he may find that he wants to change it.

Of course, this may never happen, and then the counsellor is faced with the choice as to whether to tell him bluntly about his fault, or to hope that at some later date he will discover it for himself. It is here that pastoral counsellors will frequently part company. Some lean towards the directive approach and are of the opinion that when a moral issue is involved it is their duty to make it clear to the person. Others feel that they should follow the non-judgemental principle of counselling, and wait. The former will usually qualify their attitude with a theological argument related to sin, repentance and forgiveness; the latter will trust that when the conscience of the person has developed or revived sufficiently he will accept as his own the values and standards which the counsellor will have tacitly suggested to him in the course of counselling.

Jung hints that it is not essential to indicate to a person that he is doing wrong, for 'there appears to exist something which may be called the conscience of the human race, which metes out its own punishment to everyone who does not somewhere, at some time, restrain his pride in his own virtue and abstain from self-justification by making a confession of his shortcomings ... it is as if the unreserved confession throws me into the arms of humanity. It frees me from the burden of moral exile'.[8] Thus it seems that there exists in our being, regardless of our religious standpoint and independent of our church communion, a need to articulate not only our misfortunes, but also our mistakes and failures.

Some counsellors are of the opinion that there is no specific value in mentioning God or religious doctrines in counselling, since God works through human relationships. This would be so if the purpose of such counselling was simply to adjust a person in his relationships with other people and the surroundings in which he finds himself. But pastoral counselling does imply a meaningful relationship not only with other people, but with God as well. Therefore most pastoral counsellors do feel that at some point the person must be helped to become increasingly aware of the spiritual side of his nature.

Donald D. Evans, writing on 'Pastoral Counselling and Traditional Theology' in the *Scottish Journal of Theology* puts this very clearly. 'Where a person is in a situation of psychological threat and accepts only those interpretations which enable him to evade his real problem, it is usually useless and sometimes dangerous to present Christian doctrine. Non-directive therapy may help him to gain the self-knowledge which leads to mental health and maturity; pastors may use it as part of their healing in such cases. When this stage is reached, there is a place for rational discussion or persuasion concerning doctrine'.[9] The counsellor's most difficult decision is to know when to speak and when to keep silent, when to lead, and when to refrain from leading.

The stage at which the counsellor will be able most readily to introduce religious ideals will be in the process of growth or re-education, when the person has begun to understand himself and his motives, and is trying, with the help of the counsellor to re-orientate his life in accordance with the new discernment which he has reached about himself. Non-directive counselling would not involve indoctrination, but it would permit encouragement on the part of the counsellor to enable the person to understand the counsellor's own attitudes and values. This is perhaps where many non-pastoral counsellors fail, for they are able to reach the root of a person's troubles and to help him to rid himself of some of his conflicts and anxieties, but they are able to offer little to put in their place. The pastoral counsellor has something to offer in this respect and he should be aware of this.

Part of his task is to help the person to reach a relationship with God, for he believes that only in this way can the person be completely whole. Faith can never be given. The counsellor has to help the person to develop his own faith, and this faith is not necessarily identical with that of the religious group to which the counsellor belongs. It is the form of faith that brings the person into touch with God, and depends very much upon the background and personality of the person himself. When a person arrives at an insight into himself and his own experiences, he also arrives at an insight into the experiences of others and into the way in which God works in human life. He is ready to find faith for himself and it is the counsellor's job to help him to do so.

This aspect of the work of the pastoral counsellor is by no means finished when a relationship with God has been reached. In fact it has only just begun. He has now to help the person to cherish this relationship and to grow within it – what Christianity terms 'growing in grace'. This may prove a difficult and tedious proceeding particularly if the relationships, which the person has had previously with God and with others, have never been lasting or successful.

The first step is learning to love and this is possible since the person has now reached a positive approach to life. Love is much more than simply tender feelings. It is a strong emotion, capable of service and sacrifice for those for whom affection is felt. In general human relationships it is expressed in firm friendliness, and in the considerate care for those who are the objects of our affections. In the life of the community it shows itself as a capacity for genuine public spirit and disinterested endeavour for the welfare of the whole. This going out of oneself and giving of oneself to others is only possible if the person is secure and stable within, and so it is only when he has dealt with his own internal fears and conflicts that a person can begin to develop this capacity to love.

It is here that the personality of the counsellor is of the utmost importance, for it is through the way in which he reveals the meaning of love that the person can learn something of it. If he has shown this sort of love throughout the whole process of counselling, then the person is more likely to begin to understand it, and to learn a little of what it means. As the person begins to grow in love and in an understanding of its deeper meaning, it is possible to introduce some of the other characteristics of maturity. The counsellor has to use his example and his ingenuity to develop an understanding of such things as joy, peace, patience, faithfulness and self-discipline.

The counsellor who is also a pastor has the resources of religion to offer the person in order to help him to maintain and develop the integration of his personality. These include prayer and the scriptures, as well as the sacraments and rites of the church. If he uses these resources, he needs to remember that he is passing from pastoral counselling to pastoral care, and the extent to which he does this will depend very much on any previous acquaintance the person has had with them. It is important that the counsellor should not press them upon anyone. An allusion to their usefulness and help in the counsellor's own life is often the best way of introduction, and this can lead on to a greater discussion as to how they may help in fostering a sense of security and stability and in bringing a person more fully into relationship with other people and with God. Respect for a person involves his freedom to choose his own way of knowing and worshipping God. Therefore it sometimes happens that, at this stage, a counsellor may find it more satisfactory to suggest to the person that he should find some other spiritual adviser whose approach is more akin to his own way of thinking.

If the counsellor is in charge of a church he has at his disposal unique resources for helping a person who has reached this stage of progress towards maturity. In a church which is alive to the importance of relationships, its members will be related to God before they are related to one another, and related to each other because they are related to God. This sort of double relationship should lead to an open and accepting community and one which is ready to take in the outsider and make him one of themselves. Its group solidarity will offer the sort of social identification which people with problems are often lacking and which is desperately needed for their recovery. The counsellor can then, at the right moment, add to his personal form of help the benefits which arise from being a member of a close and understanding group of people, and when counselling comes to its natural end the person will still have the support of the group.

If the pastoral counsellor is to be adept at his job, he cannot expect to do all this without some sort of training, even though it may be slight and self-taught. Some reading about methods of counselling, combined with writing up and studying his contacts with parishioners or those whom he helps in the course of his daily work in hospital, youth club or other organisation will teach him a great deal. But it is always better if he can meet with others to discuss the conclusions he reaches or, if it is possible, to study cases together and see how each would respond to some particular situation. This is not only useful in discovering satisfactory ways of helping people, but it also shows a counsellor that his own reactions to certain types of people and their problems are not necessarily the only valid and reasonable ones.

The method followed in this type of meeting is usually that of studying cases which one or other of the members have found difficult, interesting or illustrative of some point that they have been thinking about. Sometimes tape-recordings are used, and this has the advantage of indicating intonations of voice and pauses which are not indicated in the reported case. But it can only be done with the permission of all those present at the interview which is recorded, and the knowledge that it is being recorded does tend to cramp the style of the participants and to take some of the spontaneity away from the interview.

More formal teaching in pastoral counselling is not easy to find in Britain at the present time. There are academic courses linked with psychology and sociology at some of the universities, though these are directed more to pastoral work than specifically to counselling. Then there are smaller groups, such as the Richmond Fellowship and the National Association for Mental Health, which offer short or intermittent courses for those interested in the helping services. Some of these courses are specifically for those dealing with highly disturbed people, but others provide a more general understanding of the human personality, so that those who attend may be more aware of the difficulties of communication with other people and may learn how to reach an easier relationship with them.

Clinical theology courses, which have appeared in many parts of the country in the last few years, attempt to teach pastoral counselling with some knowledge of depth psychology and to link this with theological concepts. They use the medical approach and so are useful for those who are working in hospitals and prisons. But a very firm grasp of the rather complicated diagrams and explanations has to be achieved if those studying in this manner are not to gain a superficial knowledge. Many clergy and others who have attended the courses have been greatly helped by this approach, and it has brought them into a far closer touch with the needs of those they are trying to help. There is, however, the danger that where there is lack of depth the concepts may be used indiscriminately or at the wrong time, and this can cause untold harm to the insecure and immature personality. Those interested in counselling could learn much from attending courses in casework, though it is not easy to do, for such courses are mostly restricted to those training for social work and form a part of a more comprehensive study. A deeper understanding of personal relationships is provided by organisations such as the Tavistock Institute, where the emphasis is primarily upon psychotherapy. This, again, is useful for those who are working with disturbed people, but it can be somewhat advanced and complicated for the ordinary counsellor who is usually meeting the reasonably balanced person at some period of difficulty or strain.

The essential thing for the pastoral counsellor is to be able to make the right sort of relationship with the person he is counselling, and so the type of training he will choose will depend very much on the needs of his own personality and upon the sorts of people who are likely to come to him. Since everyone has traits of character and blind spots, it is necessary to be aware of these to become a successful counsellor. Therefore the question sometimes arises as to whether the counsellor should undergo personal therapy as a part of his training. This may help some people, although it is not usually necessary, and it can be both costly and time-consuming.

Perhaps the best way in which the pastoral counsellor can equip himself for the job is to take the form of training which is most congenial to him, and which seems to prepare him best for the work he has to do. His training is not only the learning of techniques and the ways of dealing with different types of people. It lies primarily within himself. For the successful pastoral counsellor is not necessarily the person who has all the practical knowledge at his fingertips. He is the person whose attitude to life and to other people reveals the tremendous depth of his understanding.

VII. The Stages of the Human Life Span

The pastoral counsellor will meet people in all the various stages of human life, and these people will be entangled in the particular problems of their age group as well as having their own special problems. The way in which they will talk and listen will be conditioned by their life histories, which will be known only very imperfectly by the counsellor, and it will also be affected by the interests, emotions and problems of their particular period of growth. The counsellor must speak to their stage of development and in doing so be able to form a bridge from himself to where they are. He must therefore know the human life cycle from within, with the basic problems of each period of human growth and decline so that he can be sure of touching a sympathetic cord in each experience.

The various periods of human growth and decline each have their own needs and emotional tones and frustrations, and as such they are capable of descriptions and of handling by the counsellor. Each period contains within itself problems which are common to most people at this stage of development, although these are coloured by the personality of the person and by the accustomed ways he has acquired of dealing with his difficulties. Throughout life there is also a gradual groping towards maturity and so the importance of the needs of any section of the life cycle not only touches the relevant problems of that period, but it also involves the question of the final worth of the person. Matters of the deepest significance may lie beyond the person's psychological condition and the circumstances in which he finds himself, and within the spiritual sphere. To the pastoral counsellor a psychological understanding of human growth and development is extremely important, but it is not all-important. It is the means whereby a person can be more surely brought to an understanding of some of the circumstances in which he finds himself, and so to a deeper knowledge of the truth about himself and about God.

Throughout life the personality of the individual develops, but this development takes place at a far greater speed in the early years than later on. That is why it is so important that children should be given the right type of environment and the proper sort of care and protection when they are young. Nature has provided the child with a large number of potentialities, capacities, instincts and patterns of behaviour and intelligence which should enable him to cope with the problems and difficulties of life and all these are necessary to maintain a normal and adequate form of existence. The aim therefore should be to provide the fullest opportunity for the development and use of all these capacities.

The first few years of life are the crucial ones with regard to the child's personality. Of these, the first two are engaged in the emergence of the primitive instincts and potentialities, such as curiosity, assertiveness and fear. The third and fourth years are occupied with the organisation and harmonisation of these various impulses under the control of the will. The foundations of the adult personality are thus laid down in these early years.

If the child's personality is well organised, that is if the impulses are fully expressed and usefully directed, then he will tend to be happy in disposition, strong in will and of good character. But if on the other hand there is a failure in organisation during these early years, the person as he grows up may be incapable of facing the responsibilities of life and may fall a victim to various disorders. That is why many of the predisposing causes of neurotic disorders originate in these first three or four years. Later events such as a shock, an illness or an unhappy marriage may precipitate an actual breakdown, but these experiences might not have produced such an illness if the person had not been predisposed by unhappy conditions in childhood.

The new born baby is totally dependent on the care and attention of others and without this he could not survive. Everything has to be done for him and he himself can contribute nothing. He has an extraordinarily restricted environment. At first his whole world consists of his own body, and only gradually does he come to realise that there are things and people around him. Then his world begins to expand and he starts to explore it. He has no previous experience to help in these explorations, but he soon discovers from the attitude of those around him that there are things he may do, and may not do. These will often conflict with what he wants and so this brings him up against the concept of frustration which he will meet with throughout his life. This experience of frustration is extremely important in infancy and childhood and it is absolutely inevitable and impossible to avoid. It is an integral part of growing up, of character development and of personality formation. The child will not like frustration any more than an adult does, but the way in which he deals with it will have far-reaching results.

Every infant, perfectly rightly and naturally, has a primitive demand for his own physical and emotional desires and needs. What he has to discover is the degree to which he can adapt himself to other things which are equally inevitable, that is the family, the group and the community in which he lives. Looked at in this way it is quite obvious that there are many people who go through infancy, childhood and even into adult life without ever growing past the stage of wanting things entirely their own way. They do not feel that the community has any right to make demands on them, or make them conform in any way, because they have not learnt the need to give and take. These are the people who in infancy and childhood have not grown through the stage of learning how to cope with frustration and their demands are still, so to speak, at an infantile level. If, on the other hand, the infant and then the child is handled suitably, he will learn to accept the frustrations that life inevitably brings. As an adult he will still feel the infantile response to frustration, but he will know how to deal with these feelings and work them out in ways that are socially acceptable and useful.

If the frustrations of life are to be accepted by the infant and later by the child, they will have to have two very important characteristics. In the first place the frustration which is experienced must be reasonable and not excessive for the level of development that has been reached, and secondly the experience must come in a setting in which the infant or child feels basically secure and wanted. Hence the importance first of all of the care of the mother, and then of good relationships with other members of the family.

The development and control of the emotions are closely connected with this. In infancy moods swing very rapidly from one extreme to another, from tears to hilarious laughter and from anger and hate to love. But gradually the child learns to control them to some extent so that they fit into the needs of the family and the community. The emotions of adult life are very much the same as those of infancy, but they have become more controlled, less dramatic and more closely connected with events.

The infant will also begin to develop his capacity to form relationships. It takes him a time to recognise other people around him. At first he views them as part of himself and only gradually comes to realise that they are separate possessions, to which he develops a taking rather than a giving relationship. Then he begins to see that his father and mother are not solely his possessions but have a relationship with each other. He realises that relationships are not exclusive, but have to be shared. As he begins to recognise the interrelationship between his parents he begins to pattern himself on the parent of the same sex, and not only to copy the behaviour of this parent, but also to form his first picture of masculinity and femininity. Thus it is not only important how parents handle their children, but also what sort of people they appear to the child to be. If the parents are mature and capable of coping with the difficulties of life, then the child will have a better chance of laying the foundations of maturity.

This situation may be complicated by the absence of one or other of the parents. The mother may be dead or have deserted, or the father away for long periods on account of his work. A similar sort of thing happens, of course, if a mother cannot be motherly or a father fatherly. The child is handicapped in the necessary stage of learning to share relationships and sort out the concepts of masculinity and femininity, for he cannot use as a pattern a parent with whom he has virtually no relationship, whether or not that parent is actually present in the household. If this foundation is missing, then the subsequent capacity to form relationships may be harmed. The child may find it more difficult to get on with his brothers or sisters, with his school mates, at work and in the community. And so he grows up into a 'difficult' person. He may become resentful, argumentative, sullen or hostile, and may not be particularly likeable until the causes for this are understood.

As the child grows older, his image or pattern of the adult becomes modified by his relationships with other adults and so becomes more composite and complex. Teachers, relatives and friends will play an important part in this. He will gradually build up within himself a composite image of the good person whom he should try to please, and try to be like, and the ways in which he deals with his frustrations, his anxieties and his conflicts will bear some correspondence with this image.

Childhood is often referred to as the latency period, for it is relatively free from the emotional outbursts of the infant and toddler. It is a stage of rapid physical growth, of learning and of social development. Adolescence, on the other hand, is quite as far reaching a change as that from infancy to childhood, and it is attended by considerable turmoil and difficulty. Most of these difficulties are normal and inevitable, but if they are not understood they can cause much distress to both adolescent and to parents.

Three important things happen with the adolescent. First of all there comes a doubting of authority, a rebellion against it and a tendency to feel that any kind of adult authority must automatically be questioned. The reaction may vary from frank rebellion to a sullen, resentful, disgruntled attitude to authority. There may be a belief that the adolescent automatically knows what is right and proper to do, and that adults are necessarily wrong in their ideas. Secondly, there is a seeking of new experience and new activities which may change almost as soon as they are begun. This is a major factor behind the wastage of youth clubs, since many join on the crest of a new enthusiasm only to drift away to something else soon afterwards. Thirdly, there is the physical development of puberty. Adolescence is a time of great physical growth and physical changes, each with its accompanying emotion, partly exciting and partly frightening. Many feel torn between the urge to explore these new feelings, and the prohibitions of their own super-ego and the influences of their parents, teachers and other adults. The adolescent is in a very difficult situation in our culture, for physically he is an adult, and perhaps economically too if he has started work, but in terms of social development he cannot possibly have grown into a mature adult. If he is still at school, or is a student, he is still treated in many respects as a child, despite his adult attributes. There is therefore a great deal of anxiety aroused by all this uncertainty and by these far-reaching changes, and the ways in which such anxieties are handled are very important in his subsequent behaviour as an adult.

The period of adolescence is difficult for adults as well, for they have to learn to give up the old parent-child relationship and substitute a more permissive approach. The role of the adult changes from one of control to one of guiding and of helping the young person to grow through this difficult stage without getting too much hurt in the process. Adult society as a whole tends to be critical and even hostile to the adolescent, partly perhaps because it subconsciously wishes it were young again and partly because it finds it different to remember the attitudes of adolescence. It has to learn to accept the changes of adolescence and to adapt to them.

The widening of the social contacts of the adolescent will vary with individual and cultural differences of experience and opportunity, yet they will frequently follow the same general pattern of development. In the earlier years of the period the characteristic social group is a small homogeneous one of the same sex and age. This will gradually change into the small group of both sexes, and only beyond this stage is it common to see the same boy and girl regularly together and away from the group of both sexes. Often, too, the first chosen individual partner will be picked from outside the original group.

A stable relationship with a person of the opposite sex will usually materialise and this will be the precursor to marriage, though it may be some time before this relationship is found, and marriage will often take place without such a stable relationship. The good financial position of the young today makes marriage possible at an earlier age, and also after only a short acquaintance, during which the two young people have had very little opportunity of getting to know one another.

Marriage itself always requires adjustment, particularly in the realms of sex, finance, responsibility for the home and the sharing of all the routine of living together. But contemporary marriage introduces special strains. The roles of men and women are not well defined and stable, so that it is often difficult to reach a decision as to where the authority and control lies. This is further complicated when the newly married are unable to have a home of their own, for then the existing stresses of the different generations serve to exacerbate the difficulties of early marriage adjustment.

The coming of a child introduces a further difficulty for it causes a triangular relationship. It may often act as a binding force between husband and wife because it represents their togetherness. But on the other hand it may be a strain upon their relationship since it means that they have less time to care for one another. They are now parents, and latent insecurity may come to the fore, especially if the child is difficult or shows a marked preference for one of the parents. Jealousies may be aroused which will have their effect both upon the child and upon the parents themselves.

There is usually a need for more than one child to keep the balance in family relationships and most families consist of two or three. As a family grows there develop numerous jealousies and hates as well as love and devotion. Children react to one another with mixed feelings, and so do parents to their children. New sets of relationships are constantly being formed within the family.

A family is therefore a living, extremely sensitive organism in which every change of feeling in any one member inevitably produces emotional reactions in all the others. In the development of the child the nature of the marital relationship of the parents is of enormous importance. It will make all the difference to the child's sense of security whether each parent accepts his or her role as husband or wife with the maximum degree of comfort, or whether the relationship is used for the mutual feeding of neurotic needs. The child will also play some part in their relationship, for very early in life the child finds ways of exerting some control on his environment, and of building up defences, responses and behaviour patterns that in his experience are guaranteed to secure for him the parental love and acceptance he needs.

A new kind of adjustment is needed on the part of the parents when the children leave home, for then there is a vacuum in the life of the family and a feeling that the better years of life are ending. Sometimes there is an impulse to recapture youth which will shake a sound and successful marriage. In other cases all that the partners have gone through together will give a more positive meaning to marriage. Nevertheless, adjustment is not easy and may pass through many difficult phases before it is finally achieved.

Old age brings the family to its final test. The increased loss of strength and other physical complications may lead to physical and psychological difficulties. Yet each individual retains intense feelings of his individuality and independence. This will often necessitate a change in relationship between parents and children. An adult married child will have responsibilities for aged parents, but also to the immediate family. As the old person gradually loses his powers, so further adjustments will have to be made which may reactivate all early good and bad feelings between parents and children. Many elderly parents and adult children are forced together, not because they necessarily want to, but because anything else seems worse. Modern society creates a real conflict for the middle-aged children of elderly parents.

Thus the cycle of family life waxes and wanes between dependence and independence. The baby who is dependent becomes the independent adult, but in old age and death he is dependent again. The way babies are brought up and the way old people die are deeply interrelated, not only because babies will become old and dependent themselves, but because the feelings that they will acquire in infancy and childhood will be carried over into old age and often be far stronger then than before. Parents usually wish better things for their children than they had themselves and will take inordinate care to see that something they disliked intensely does not happen to their children. This will not necessarily benefit the children. In fact it can have quite the opposite effect. Or if parents have been hurt too much by being caught between the responsibility for their children and their parents, they may do all they can to make things different for their own children, and this will not bring success either. The counsellor has always to be aware of this ebb and flow of life, and of the extent to which there is interdependence between its different periods.

Modern counselling often tends to forget this, and to proceed as though a person were isolated from all the interrelationships of family life. The basic cause for a person's difficulties undoubtedly lies in the early years of his life and with the ways in which he was enabled to deal with his conflicts and frustrations. But the present form and degree of his difficulties are very closely related to his position within the family and to the relationships which this evokes. Counselling is a far more complicated process than it appears, and its dimensions are manifold. Therefore, although it is necessary to consider counselling as it applies to the different age groups and their relevant problems, it has always to be remembered that there is no real separation and that what has happened at a previous period may have important implications for the present.

COUNSELLING THE YOUNG

The family, as the cradle of human relationships, has always been important. It offers its members an education for living so that the adjustments which are worked out within the family are transferable to other relationships. Many of the difficulties which arise in family relationships today are the result of the fact that each new generation is now forced to improvise instead of being able to lean largely on generations of tested experience. The tendency is now to make the children the centre, and to overlook the chain reaction which exists between children, parents and grandparents.

The child needs guidance as it passes through the different phases of its early life, and this is provided by a variety of people

I

— the parents, the teacher, the parson, the youth leader and quite often the vocational guidance service. It is this haphazard sort of counselling, usually at a period of crisis, which distinguishes the ways in which we help our young people in this country from the more formalised methods adopted on the American continent. There childcare counselling, usually with the family as a group, has contact with a child from a very early age.

Counselling the young in this country, when it has not been left entirely to the parents, has always been the duty of the clergy and ministers, especially in churches where such rites as confirmation tend to take place at the beginning of adolescence. Such counselling is usually both moral and religious, with the twin purpose of helping the young person to appreciate the difference between 'right' and 'wrong', and also of educating him in the doctrines of the particular denomination to which he will belong. Only very rarely are the problems of relationship, which are frequently the deepest problems which the child of this age has, sympathetically considered.

The very young child does not need the forms of help which counselling provides, for up to the eighth year of his life he has unity. He believes in good and has absolute faith and trust in his mother, even if she is weak and bad. It is when separation from his mother begins, and he sets out to fend for himself as an individual through association with his equals in the 'gang' that some help may be needed. The child at this stage desires – above all – experience, and especially of being able to affect people and things. Thus far he has followed the attitudes learnt from his parents, but now he begins to become aware of a much wider range of behaviour which provides obvious enjoyment and excitement.

Individual counselling at this stage is rarely of great help. But the child will learn much from his contact with the group and from the example of some older person who to him appears in the role of a hero. This is the period when scouts, guides and similar activities are suitable and when the child through participation in such groups learns to extend his own small moral code and to adopt attitudes which are likely to become basic to his future life. He may not understand much of any moral or religious teaching which he receives, but he will feel the atmosphere of the group to which he belongs, and of the personality of the leader.

All children will find some difficulty in adjustment at this period but where the interpersonal relationships in the family are unsound then these difficulties may be more marked. For instance, when parents constantly disagree and seem to be irreconcilable the children are likely to have an attitude of hopelessness regarding any possibilities in life. Disagreement will also affect the parent-child relationship for when parents are at loggerheads with each other they frequently draw one child to themselves and by living for him make this child compulsively dependent. Similarly, when mothers have no identity except by means of the children they tend to love them for what they do for them rather than for what they are. Thus the reactions and behaviour of the parents during the critical growing stages of the children's lives are likely to have far-reaching future effects, and may even be the cause of hysterical and depressive illnesses when the children reach adulthood.

A counsellor will often have to deal with parent-child relationship problems, and then it is very difficult to decide when it is best to stay with the projection of the difficulty upon the child, or when to move into an examination of a marital problem which is usually present as well. A course which is frequently chosen is to start with the marital problem, and when some change in this takes place to see if it has any effect upon the child. Greater mutuality and stability in the relationships of parents may give them the understanding and the urge to take a deeper interest in the problems of the child.

When this does not happen, there is always the possibility of help from the child guidance clinics. The widespread and increasing use of such clinics for troubled children is closely linked with the knowledge that the origin of much neurotic illness lies in impaired family relationships, and the hope that early treatment can prevent or postpone such adult illness. Methods which are frequently used in these clinics are to take the child's side in interviews so that he may become relatively independent of the family and home environment, and to encourage the child to relax and to act out his problems with the help of such things as games or painting, which may reveal unusual noisy and aggressive behaviour. The pastoral counsellor is not equipped to take part in this, but he is often needed to explain the methods and their outcome to bewildered and distracted parents.

Counselling services for the child at school has for some time been a usual feature in American education. Though the counsellor is primarily concerned with educational choices, at the same time he has an important function as a general adviser to the student and as a sort of moral tutor. He helps to resolve personal problems of family or school relationships, difficulties of study or financial need, and also concerns himself with the numerous questions which trouble adolescents during the growing-up process. The American counsellor will find himself giving sex education, or marriage guidance, or even the kind of general advice which consists of listening to somebody's problems, and he will reinforce much of what he says by psychological tests and reference to other specialists when this is necessary.

Traditionally the form teacher or the housemaster has undertaken the pastoral care of his or her pupils in this country, and in those schools which have been fortunate enough to have a full-time chaplain, this has been his job. But however good the relationship a teacher or chaplain has with the pupils, the role is necessarily restricted by the position of authority, and so any counselling done will tend to be affected. Therefore it is becoming more usual to invite an outsider, often one trained in social casework or in the educational work of the Marriage Guidance

Council, to meet small groups in order to discuss the more usual problems and to talk with any who want personal help.

Usually it is the adolescent who will bring problems to the school counsellor, and these are often worries about sexual development and moodiness, conflicts with parents over leisure time activities, anxieties over appearance or about the way to behave in a new situation. There is either too rigid parental control or none at all, or perhaps inconsistency. Sometimes the parents are unhappily married; they may use violence; there may be financial worries or over-crowding, or aged grandparents adding to the strain of family relationships. Rivalries between brothers and sisters also cause many hard feelings. A spoilt younger child, the unfair distribution of family chores, a handicapped brother or sister, a twin, a large family spread over many years in which there seems no place for the youngest member or too much responsibility for the first-born. School problems include such things as worries about school work, strong feelings about unjust punishment, or school regulations, or perhaps a group problem as to how to handle a trouble-maker or one who is always fighting. A girl may feel that no one loves or respects her and that it is quite impossible to make any lasting relationships.

The main job of the counsellor, as in all forms of counselling, is to help the young person to recognise his problem himself. He will usually feel friction or frustration but not be fully aware of its cause. The counsellor has, perhaps by the use of some leading questions, to make him recognise this. He has then to decide what to do about it, and this requires some training in independence and decision making. Thus it is often helpful to do much of the educational work of counselling in small groups, and to deal privately with the particular problem.

Overall concern is most important, and this involves considering the person in his social context. Therefore the counsellor has to have some knowledge not only of his school situation, but also of that of his family and his friends. It may imply what the social worker would regard as a case history, and this cannot be obtained quickly or without a degree of trouble. Much counselling of the young fails here, because the counsellor has not been in a position where he was fully aware of all the circumstances.

Continuity is another requisite for the adequate counselling of the young. The young person should be able to contact the same person over a long period of time, so that a relationship between him and the counsellor of sufficient depth and trust can be established. This is so often difficult to achieve, for a clergyman may leave the parish, a child may change school or move to another district and the continuity will be difficult to maintain.

The counsellor will not usually be able to meet these demands unless he can call upon the collective resources of the school, the home and perhaps the youth club to help him. He will need understanding and support from them and their co-operation in helping the young person to follow the chosen course of action. Much of this will depend upon an adequate knowledge of the social services within the area and of the personalities of those who work with them. This may include such social workers as the health visitor, the probation officer, the child-care officer, the youth leader and the N.S.P.C.C. inspector.

In this country, voluntary organisations play some part in counselling young people. An example is 'Amici', an association of parents who have come together to provide counsel for young people between the ages of seventeen and twenty-four, many of them students. The underlying theory is that the family is not today a self-sufficient, viable unit, and that young people need and are entitled to find help and guidance outside their own families, such as their predecessors might have found among the members of the extended family. Those who come to 'Amici' are treated as friends of the family and their problems discussed in an informal but absolutely confidential manner. The basic function of the counsellors is to listen, so that the younger people can talk exhaustively, free from the emotional tensions of their own family circle. Counsellors are expected to react as experienced parents, taking a commonsense, practical view of a problem and to give constructive suggestions to help their young visitors to overcome a problem which threatens to be too much for their own unaided effort, or to refer them to someone else if there is a need for specialist advice. The very informality of this association, where counselling often takes place in a member's house, is able to help young people who for a variety of reasons shy away from other agencies, or feel that they should be in far worse difficulties before seeking outside help. By limiting its membership to parents, 'Amici' ensures that in assisting young people the interests of their own parents and other family ties will not be forgotten. This approach is thought to be nearer to the real needs of young people than some planned form of counselling.

The counsellor, who is also a pastor, will find that in adolescence the young person is ready for spiritual counselling. Often quite suddenly the child seems to apprehend the spiritual ideals and support offered him by religion. Up to this time he has lived largely by an inherited natural pattern as far as his religious impulses are concerned. It often seems that children become aware, however dimly, of the existence of God before they have any conscious need of him. It is at this stage that he will need the help of expert counselling to enable him to realise something of the reality of God so that he may be saved from two very common pitfalls which can lead to severe mental conflict, that of going to God only when in need and so regarding Him as an indulgent parent; or of making a complete split between the natural and the spiritual. Adolescence is the period when tensions come, causing disruption and suffering and there is the need for the personality to survive as a unity and to become mature. Here religion has an important part to play by bringing a balance between those things which are of the body, mind and spirit. Counselling is not easy, for much depends upon whether the child has had love, security and good images in the earlier years, and what sort of religious instruction he has received. It is usually fatal to exploit conversion in those with no religious background. As in all counselling, the counsellor has to be able to offer the reality of God in terms of the young person's own experience and background and this will vary vastly from one young person to another. Similarly no particular church or denomination is likely to be suitable for all. Each young person has to choose, and his choice will depend on many things, such as his upbringing, his experience in some particular church, his friends, and the personality of the pastor or minister. This could cause difficulty when the counsellor is himself an ordained man, who would recommend his own form of religion. But the counsellor has a duty to be impartial for it is the young person himself who has to make the choice. It can always be suggested that he try some particular church, and make a change if he does not feel at home. The good counsellor should have the confidence of his young people so that they will feel able to consult him if they want to make a change and if they do, it is imperative that the counsellor should help to make the change easy and successful.

One of the most important problems which any counsellor has to meet with the adolescent is that of sexual relationships. The difficulty in this area of life today is that of uncertainty. People do not know what to believe, to do, or to teach, and hence the confusion. Much of the teaching on love that is recommended today, especially in recent theology, suggests a far greater freedom than in the past, and this is commendable in that it gets away from the old abhorrence of sexuality. The counsellor has to be able to suggest a positive approach to love, and this is difficult when the word 'love' has so many meanings. There are numerous variations on the theme, such as longing, lusting, desiring, yearning, self-expression and even self-giving, but none is entirely adequate to express the loving relationship of God which should be repeated in a person's relationship with another. The most that any counsellor can do is to be sure about his own attitude, and this sense of conviction should help the young person to make up his own mind and be definite about any line of action he chooses.

It is only comparatively recently that sex and marriage have been discussed by young people before they had made their choice of marriage partner. Now youth clubs of all types and an increasing number of schools are encouraging this, and the Marriage Guidance Council is devoting far more of its time and finances to this aspect of their work. Counselling of this nature falls into two forms, the normal educational work among young people, and the preparation for marriage of those who are already engaged.

Many people are ignorant or only partially informed about the so-called facts of life and about the practical aspects of boy-girl relationships and of marriage. It is the function of those concerned with their welfare to see that this is provided and the usual method is in group discussion in co-operation with youth leaders, teachers and local authorities. These young people will often reveal anxieties and problems to the group leader which they could not readily share with their parents and teachers. Sometimes this is possible in the group if the problem can be stated in general terms, but when a young person has brought a problem to him privately after a group discussion individual counselling on the part of the leader is necessary. The role of the leader then becomes that of helping the young person to arrive responsibly at his own decision, and not to prescribe a pattern of living for him. This is the distinction between moral education and moral instruction, which is so often provided by the churches. In the former the young person is helped to reach his own decisions upon personal relationships in the light of what he knows. In the latter the decisions have already been made for him and he is expected to follow them.

Pre-marital counselling is both a need for information and for resolving some of the anxieties which normally surround the sex relationship, particularly with young people who take life and their responsibilities seriously. Information can, of course, be provided by a book or booklet, but coupled with personal discussion it can be far more helpful, particularly if the discussion helps the two engaged people to talk to each other, not in a clinically accurate way but rather as a means of conveying to each other how they feel and what puzzles them or worries them.

Most clergy interview engaged couples before marriage, and it should be possible for work of this nature to be done by them. But a girl would often prefer to talk to a woman counsellor and at a private interview rather than with her fiancé, and although counsellors may not feel reserved at interviewing an engaged person of either sex, the person being interviewed may well feel embarrassed and so not be able to bring up the personal anxieties that concern him or her.

These anxieties can be very varied, though they usually centre round intercourse. Sometimes it is a fear of not being able to be successful and so to lose prestige in the eyes of the other partner. But even when sexual intercourse has already been experienced there may still be anxiety over not being able to integrate sexuality with love and affection. Problems such as these lie at the basis of many future difficulties in marriage, and it is a pity that the churches, where the majority of the marriages still take place, have not become sufficiently aware of this and made proper provision for counsellors of both sexes to be available to talk with those who are about to be married.

Two other problems will often come up in pre-marital counselling. The first is the perennial one of the in-laws, which is far better dealt with at this stage than later on. Marriage always means a breaking away from home, but what really matters is whether the emotional ties that remain are still those of childhood, or whether they have become those of a more mature outlook.

The counsellor has to help them both to reach this sort of relationship. It is no good advising different kitchens or even different houses, if the psychological dependence is still there.

A second problem with which a counsellor is often faced is the dilemma as to whether to break off an engagement because of some deep disagreement, or 'lovers' quarrel'. There are many reasons for this happening and the period of engagement is intended to provide time for the two people to discover whether they are really suited to one another. Such a quarrel often occurs when one of the young people suddenly perceives the other as he or she really is, without the glamour that surrounds their relationship. Such a testing time will inevitably arrive, and it is better before than after marriage. When two people can see themselves as they really are and accept one another there is the possibility of much future happiness, but when this involves a broken engagement the agony of feeling which comes from being rejected and alone can be intense. There counselling of a supportive type has an important part to play.

MARRIAGE COUNSELLING

Unhappy parents provide unhappy homes. Children grow up in these unhappy homes and in later life provide unhappy homes for other children. This has long been recognised and disharmony in marriage has been deplored by psychologists, sociologists, clergymen, physicians, psychiatrists, educators, lawyers and social workers. Marriage counselling has been carried on by interested individuals in all these professional groups, and also in this country by the National Marriage Guidance Council which trains carefully selected people in the skills needed for marriage guidance. The local marriage guidance counsellor, whose work is entirely voluntary and unpaid, now works as a member of a team with the support of professional tutors and consultants who give their services to the local marriage guidance council.

Until recently counselling has tended to concentrate on symptoms of marital disturbance, such as the inability to budget and unsatisfactory sex relationships. It was not considered part of professional responsibility to seek out and treat the disturbed personality patterns of individual partners which might be the underlying cause of conflicts. Psychotherapists who were treating married persons were not particularly concerned about the effects of the therapy on the marriage, and tended to concentrate on the treatment of the disturbed personality pattern of the individual and to regard the stability of the marriage as outside their professional responsibility.

It is now becoming realised that marriage is not a device that a technician can mend or service, but that it is a most intricate and sensitive relationship of personalities and of the external pressures to which they are exposed. Marriage is the closest of all human adult relationships and in it the personalities of husband and wife impinge directly and constantly on each other. Its central core is love in all its variations, and its greatest hazards are hostility and anxiety. The quality of the individual's capacity to love and his ways of handling his hostilities play a central role in every marriage. Anger and hatred are bound to be present from time to time, and if they are not expressed overtly they will lie beneath the surface and may cause untold trouble. No two people are so completely matched that there is never frustration, and whenever frustration exists hostility is present; but the degree and manner of its expression vary enormously. Likewise in every marriage there will be aspects of maturity and immaturity whose needs will be expressed or gratified. Childish dependence can often emerge in times of personal stress, even between husbands and wives whose relationships are those of adult interdependence.

There is no one pattern of marriage adjustment. Ideal marriages seem to exist between two mature persons, but there are many successful neurotic marriages that meet the needs of both partners, and also many combinations of immature persons which hold well together. If the needs of the two partners dovetail well the marriage usually lasts. There may be loud complaints from one or other of the partners, and yet they will be averse to any change.

Nearly always a person in marital difficulties comes to a counsellor to ask for advice and expects to be given some definite solution to his troubles. The counsellor usually has to make it quite clear in the first interview that this is not the aim of marriage counselling, and that it is only by working through the difficulties together that any improvement will appear in the marriage relationships. Even then the counsellor will often have to make some positive suggestions if the person is to return for a second interview.

The real need in any conflict is to understand its underlying nature. This is particularly the case with emotional conflicts such as jealousy, nagging and in-law interference. Advice to stop nagging, to return to one's spouse, to be more pleasant, understanding or cheerful, to be kinder or better tempered or more patient are all quite useless because the person cannot do it as long as the true nature of his feelings and intentions and values is not understood. People act in these ways mainly because of feelings which they do not recognise or understand and which are therefore outside their control. A skilful counsellor will help a person gradually to understand these feelings and then to try to overcome the underlying conflict.

Marriage counselling differs from other forms of counselling in that three people are involved rather than two. The ways of dealing with this situation are varied. At one time it was usual to see both partners together if this was possible, but this often led to heated argument, and it seemed better to see them singly. Some agencies send the partners to different counsellors who then confer together. Others allow one counsellor to deal with both partners but to see them both separately. And, of course, there are many cases when only one of the partners will come for counselling. There is also divided opinion as to whether the counsellor should see the people in their own home. This is never the policy of the Marriage Guidance Council, but it is often the case with the clergyman or probation officer and provided there are not other relatives or children around to pry or disturb the conversation it may help to give the counsellor some ideas as to environmental pressures. Such counselling interviews, however, are usually best conducted at some neutral place.

As with all counselling, the tool is the use of words, and with it the counsellor has to create the whole attitude and atmosphere of relaxation and insight. The first interview generates the relationship, without which it is impossible to proceed. Attempts are then made to focus on the person's feelings without necessarily accepting the truth of what is said. Listening is, as usual, very important, with the occasional interruption to clarify the possible implications of what is said, and to sense the degree of negative or positive feelings. The counsellor will want to understand why the person has come at this particular moment, what his real motive was in coming and what help he seems to need, which is often quite different from what he asks for, and the mental pictures he may have of himself and other people in his life. It may take quite a number of interviews before these things become clear, and they should never be hastened but encouraged indirectly in the course of conversation.

As the person begins to understand himself and his motives better he will usually have some suggestions as to changes which he can make in his pattern of behaviour at home. He may come to understand that he was expecting things from marriage which were impossible, or that he was making assumptions about the other partner that were far from the truth. His very understanding of this will alter his behaviour and often do much to mend the marriage. At every interview the counsellor has to be ready for anything from abuse to undue affection, for in marriage problems the emotions are very near the surface and transference and counter-transference can be very rapid. It is not always possible to explore the root causes of the trouble at once. Sometimes a person comes in great distress, his feelings have not yet been fully expressed so that he is unable to think clearly, or perhaps he has some fixed ideas in his mind that overshadow everything else. He may have practical matters which need resolving if, for instance, his wife has walked out and left him with the children. In all these cases help needs to be given and time allowed before it is possible to think over calmly the feelings that may have led to the crisis.

The sexual aspect of marriage is almost bound to arise at some time during interviews even if the counsellor is not specifically asked to give help with it. It is usually a mistake to try to separate sexual problems from other problems in marriage. In some cases, of course, only skilled physical treatment will help and then reference to a doctor is necessary, but more often than not a sexual handicap can be traced to the personalities of the persons involved. Many sexual difficulties are emotional in origin and arise largely from the earlier experiences of the people concerned. As these become gradually understood through the interviews the sexual difficulties will often disappear. In the field of sexual anxiety, reassurance soundly-based and well-timed may be helpful in relieving tension and this, in its turn, may communicate itself to the other partner thus making the whole relationship more relaxed and loving.

As far as the marriage counsellor is concerned he is dealing with people not in themselves alone, but in relation to their marriage. Where he finds that the difficulties lie not only within the marriage relationship itself but in all other relationships as well, in the person's work, his social contacts, his relationships with his family, then the counsellor is justified in wondering whether the person does not need more skilled help than he can offer. The decision as to whether a person needs the help of a psychotherapist is sometimes a very difficult one, because almost all marriage problems involve people's deepest feelings and affect their other relationships to a certain extent. The counsellor has to decide whether it is a condition which he cannot deal with adequately, and also to be able to suggest successfully to the person that professional help is needed.

The boundary between counselling and psychotherapy is often very vague. In general, a counsellor talks with a person about any aspect of the marriage which the person chooses. The counsellor tries to help him to see it all more clearly and to recognise his half-understood feelings and aims, though without pressing any matter which the person is unwilling to discuss. The conversation is always in relation to the marriage, to the feelings of both partners about the various issues confronting them, about possible lines of action and probable consequences. The counsellor does not actively investigate the unconscious feelings of the person nor, even when he is himself aware of them, does he attempt to interpret them. When this task appears necessary it is time to call in the psychotherapist.

There is also a spiritual aspect to marriage counselling, for marriage is a relationship of mind, body and spirit. The pressure of unhappiness, uncertainty or anxiety often makes a person aware of the existence of another part of life, the world of spirit or of spiritual reality which has often been neglected or ignored. It is here, in this world of man's spirit, that communication between the two personalities is sometimes possible. Beyond all the turmoil of their dilemmas, their hates and frustrations, their panic and dependence there may lie an area of calm which is found to be friendly. Thus the point of despair is often the most promising point of all, for the hopeless quest for a solution is given up, and the person just waits and finds that things are coming right. This is something that the person can learn from the counsellor, provided the counsellor is aware of it himself and is able to convey something of this spiritual reality.

This brings up the question of religion in marriage counselling, and is a matter which the counsellor who is also a pastor has to face. In his own pastoral work a clergyman is operating on a common ground of belief and commitment and is the leader and guide to those to whom he ministers. As a counsellor, however, he is in a rather different role, and this may present some difficulty. In his counselling capacity he has to help, support and comfort the person within the orbit of the person's own thoughts, feelings and beliefs which may not necessarily coincide with his own as a clergyman. As a counsellor his own religious convictions should not intrude upon the counselling interviews any more than his political beliefs. Yet he may feel that he is failing in his duties as a priest if he does not introduce what he believes is essential. The only answer one can give to this is that if a clergyman or minister intends to put over his own religious convictions, this should be made quite clear to the person from the outset, and should this not be acceptable then the person should be referred to someone else.

Marriage counsellors in secular work have similar difficulties though here they arise in connection with the person's demand for some religious clarification. The counsellor, who is also a Christian, may be able to help with this, but when it is a matter of some particular form of belief it is usually better that the person should go for this to someone in the relevant denomination. Most religious groups have those who are able to help in this way, and for the Roman Catholic there is the Catholic Marriage Advisory Council.

Marriage counsellors are by no means always successful. When they fail the marriage may hang together in a very dubious way, or it may break up. In general, marriages tend to fall apart either because they were improperly constituted in the first place, or because there are changes in the personalities of the partners which tend to wreck their marital relationship. When the situation cannot be altered then the marriage is likely to end in divorce.

Counsellors are often called upon to help those who have just divorced their partner, or been divorced themselves. As with any loss the first reaction is usually one of grief, for a part of the self seems to have died. There is a need to live through the past with its sorrows and joys with someone, and then to put the memories away. The counsellor has to help the person to accept his full share of the responsibility for the rupture. Part of this responsibility is often projected on to someone else for it is too hurtful to bear alone, and the counsellor has to work through this. There is often a feeling of guilt at having damaged someone else, or at having broken the marriage vows. This can be a very real form of guilt, and the counsellor has to help the person to accept it as such and to be able to realise that the choice which was made was not so much an absolute one as a lesser of two evils. Very rarely in any break-up of a marriage can one speak of the 'guilty partner'. One partner may have left to marry someone else, but the cause for this is usually far deeper than the actual situation which brought it about.

When the time comes to take positive steps with regard to fitting once more into the current social relationships difficulties may arise. For our society, although it no longer condemns the person who has been divorced, does not make it easy for the single person to find a niche, or to form new relationships with the opposite sex. The situation may be complicated by children of the first marriage and by financial responsibilities, particularly in the case of the man who may be having to make an allowance to his divorced wife. Nevertheless, a very large number of divorced people do remarry, and most of them are more successful the second time.

The counsellor does not stop with these practical issues, but he tries to help the person to reach a new level of integration in his personality. It is often at such a point that questions are raised about the meaning of life, and then the pastoral counsellor may have an opportunity of discussing ultimate values.

It is now time for the person to become re-orientated to his new way of life and to stand on his own feet once more.

COUNSELLING THE MIDDLE-AGED

The problems of middle age have been very widely ignored in the past. Much attention has been devoted to those of the child and of the adolescent, and almost as much to the elderly, but the general attitude to people in the middle years of life has been to assume that they have had time to discover how to cope with the troubles that life brings, and so should be capable of helping themselves at this period. In fact, except for some of the more obvious difficulties associated with the menopause in women, it has been blandly assumed that middle age has no particular problems.

In actual fact the middle years of life provide as great a challenge as those of adolescence and present problems which are very similar. In the first place there are biological changes, which are usually regarded as confined to the women. But in a much less obvious way a man may also find changes in his sexual potency in middle age which are less well recognised and because of that sometimes more surprising and more alarming.

Physical changes also take place, and may have a very deep repercussion upon the mental attitudes of the man or woman. Weight begins to increase, lines appear on the face, bifocals have to be worn and the first false teeth are introduced. There is a greying of the hair or baldness, sinews that used not to show now appear, there are scarcely discernible changes in hearing, a slight clumsiness which arises from difficulties in co-ordination and a memory that is not quite so keen as it used to be.

A person now begins to compare himself unfavourably with his more successful contemporaries. He finds that many of his ambitions and dreams have not come to pass. He can point to many injustices which have occurred and numerous occasions on which he has been done out of what he might have had. He has been so busy striving at a career or a vocation, building a home or a reputation, and engaging in all the functional aspects of living that he has given little attention to developing his cultural or his spiritual side. He is easily 'fed up' and depressed, and this is particularly the case if he has suffered from periods of depression at intervals during his earlier life.

Quite often a sense of hopelessness sets in as he thinks himself a failure economically, socially and in his intimate relationships. He begins to see himself and others in a dim and dismal light. He recognises the signs of ageing in his friends especially if he meets them after a period of time, and when he comes to look more carefully at his wife he finds that she too is growing old, and is no longer the embodiment of youth that he married. In fact all that he valued seems to be passing away and leaving him stranded to meet an unknown future.

Similar feelings assail the married woman as the middle years of life approach, though they are more likely to be more closely connected with her home and her childen. She may be having to deal with the problems of adolescents at the same time as she is trying to cope with her own problems, and this may sap her energy and warp her understanding. Or her children may have grown up and left home and she may be faced with a situation of more leisure than she knows how to occupy. Returning to her previous career or occupation is possible, but she finds herself out of date, and less able to cope with things which would have scarcely troubled her when she was younger. Part-time work of a less demanding type may be her solution, but even then there is always the nagging feeling that she has let herself down and been unsuccessful.

If she has never married, she has now to face the fact that she is unlikely to do so. Acceptance of the fact of not finding a husband is difficult in our culture where to some extent a husband provides a status value and where even today the 'spinster lady' tends to be disparaged. She may also have the practical problem of deciding whether to live alone or to find some congenial lady friend with whom to share.

The devoted daughter who has cared for her elderly parents may now have reached the time when they become a strain upon her. She usually has the two-fold task of carrying on her own job which has probably by now become more responsible, and of seeing that her mother or father is properly looked after. Sickness or absence of domestic help pose a constant problem and an uneasy sense of anxiety, and when the old person finally dies there is often a sense of guilt that more could have been done, an empty void in the home which now becomes hers, and spare time which she finds difficult to fill.

Stress and frustration are the result of all these changes and problems and a person's reactions to them depend on a great variety of factors, some of which are purely fortuitous, some idiosyncrasies of the person concerned, some the effect others have had on the person and some the contrast between what is being felt and what it is the convention or fashion to feel. But nearly always there is a mistrust and dread of middle age and an undertone of despair and defeat.

In some cultures people, when they reach middle age, gain an esteem and reverence which is rarely theirs when they are younger, and this helps to counteract some of the disadvantages which middle age inevitably brings. But in our culture this is rarely the case. It is the young people who are valued, especially those in their twenties and thirties for they are adaptable and can more easily pick up new ideas and new methods of living, and this becomes more necessary as social change takes place at an ever increasing rate. The middle aged often find themselves overlooked or pushed beyond their powers, and this can lead to many disturbances.

Some people will readily come to a counsellor to discuss these difficulties and then they will be able to work through them together in the usual manner. But many middle-aged people do not come to a counsellor because they feel that they are not expected to have difficulties and, if they do, they are thought to be quite capable of dealing with them themselves. So they will adopt various means to try to offset them or they will pretend that they do not exist.

A very usual way of doing this is to find a scapegoat and so to put the blame for the particular problem upon someone else. Quite often the blame is attributed to a particular person, a wife who is accused of not playing her part in the social round or is constantly nagging so that life becomes unbearable. Or it may be 'them', which could include anything from the government to the young people of today. The counsellor has to help the person to realise that this is not true to fact and that the difficulties really arise within the person himself. Together they will try to find out what these difficulties are, and to work some way out of them.

Another reaction is to give up the struggle and to substitute a querulous complaining about all the minor inconveniences of life and health. Sometimes there is a kind of hypochondriac apathy and tension as though the person were admitting as all too true the attitude that middle age and beyond holds nothing but defeat, humiliation and despair. The person becomes the chronic taker of medicine, the haunter of doctors' surgeries and the person who is predominantly occupied with his own bodily processes. It is usually found that most of these bodily symptoms have no organic or physical basis, and that illness is being used as a good alibi for evading the responsibility of taking an adult attitude to the process of ageing. Again the counsellor has to help the person to realise this and so to become more mature.

It often happens that this sort of thing occurs at the same time as the other marriage partner is also concerned with the difficulties of middle life. The demand on each other for sympathy can create tension and disharmony, and serve to magnify the difficulties in both cases. The one may think that his symptoms are the beginning of a serious illness which could prove fatal, and the other be quite unable to offer the sympathy and understanding which is needed at such a time.

A reaction of a very different type to this sinking into resignation or embittered defeat is to try to make some dramatic change. This may be in the form of a religious conversion, more often than not to one of the more esoteric cults which are found today. The person finds that he is able to lose his symptoms by identification with some magic or religious symbol. But more usually it takes the form of infidelity, which is sudden and compulsive and a surprise not only to the one who is deserted, but often to the person himself who follows this course. This usually happens in marriages where the partners have had some fifteen or twenty years of busy and happy married life, rather than in those which are constantly on the brink of failure.

The man who follows this course will usually look around for someone at the age of his wife when he married her, hoping that the second choice will give him his ideal. The girl whom he chooses will probably be one who finds it difficult to make relationships with her own age group and who herself is in need of the significance which such a marriage would bring her. Consciences are stilled by the attitude of his wife, whom he accuses of bickering and nagging, regardless of the fact that he himself has been partly the cause of this. What has really happened is that he is trying to revive the dreams, wishes and fantasies of his teenage or early manhood days. The trouble can be traced back far earlier in life to the time when he imagined himself as becoming the most attractive and successful person, admired and appraised by all. He tells himself that the things he wanted such as happiness, love, approval and sexual satisfactions have been denied him, because he has failed to find in his wife the fulfilment of his dream, and he now thinks that if he can begin again he will succeed.

The woman who is unfaithful is usually trying to prove that

she is still attractive and to be desired. She too may be seeking the image of her youthful lover which she has failed to find in her husband, but as a woman she is far more distressed at what she regards as her lack of physical appeal, and is flattered by the attentions of another man, who may be younger than herself. With both the man and the woman who are unfaithful the basic problem is the same, and that is the need to accept the beginning of the ageing process and to be able to adapt oneself to it.

The counsellor is generally approached by the betrayed partner, who is severely shocked emotionally. The shock may be at first an intense bewilderment and a paroxysm of anxiety which may be accompanied by a frenzied search for an explanation. At this stage the person needs someone who will be sensitive to but not unduly disturbed by violent expressions of intense unhappiness, and will listen with sympathy, understanding and kindness.

The next stage will usually be one of displacement, when what has happened will be thrown outwards or inwards, and perhaps both ways. If thrown outwards it may either take the form of intense fury against the offending partner or against someone else who seems to have been involved; or if it is cast inwards it may result in bitter self-recriminations and feelings of failure, blindness or unworthiness. In fact, it closely resembles a specially painful bereavement, for the one who is bereaved is also betrayed.

This stage is of great importance to the person concerned and needs to be handled with special care, for the counsellor will be providing something very different from what the person may have had from relatives and friends who will inevitably have taken sides and perhaps encouraged the blaming. He will be trying to help the person to understand a little of the meaning behind what has happened.

This meaning lies in the ideal picture or image which most people have of the kind of person they would like for their marriage partner. Many people recognise this and also realise that no actual person can entirely meet this fantasy. But for some people the divergence between the fantasy and the actual has never been made or acknowledged for what it is. The fantasy or image has been either ignored, dismissed, played down, sublimated or treated with contempt, with the result that its presence has only become apparent when it has been converted into human form. The greater the extent to which the fantasy has been overlooked, the more liable will the person be to place it upon someone else and mistake its identity.

The counsellor to whom such a person comes has to help him to recognise what has happened and to realise that the matter is not only a personal, emotional event on a purely relationship basis, but something far deeper and more complicated. It is an infatuation for a fantasy, and until this is recognised little can be done. Nor may it be confined to one of the marriage partners, for both may have had their fantasies and recognised them to a greater or lesser degree, and this will have coloured their reactions to one another.

Many people mistakenly think that the solution to this is to get the mind of the person on to something else so that he forgets his infatuation. Actually this is rarely possible, and if it is attempted even less likely to be successful. For the person has become the victim of an overwhelming compulsion which in some cases may make his friends and relatives think he is either depraved or mad. What the counsellor has to do is to help the person make the acquaintance of the idealised image that he has formed of the marriage partner he thinks he should have had, and to realise that he has been deceived in thinking he has found it in mortal form. The person is then able to form the image afresh with the full knowledge of his fantasy and of the many desirable attributes which the person he did marry still possesses. The other partner too needs to be aware of this, and of her own idealised images and reactions to the situation which has occurred. This is the only true reconciliation which can take place between people who have had this devastating experience, and if they can achieve it they will emerge from the experience with a greater stature, having reached as it were a new dimension in their own development and quite often in their marriage relationship.

It is the spiritual aspect of loving which the middle-aged person needs to develop if he is to find true happiness at this time of life. It is a challenge to give and receive love in a new way, in a new perspective and with a new relevance. A person will not be able to do this by following any preconceived plan, or even the path that someone else has taken. He has to discover it for himself but he need not do so alone, for his relationship with the counsellor should help him in his search. Together they will work through the emotional and complex mixed feelings until a more stable approach is reached. Then gradually, with the support of the counsellor, he will be able to discover something of the deeper and fuller meaning of love.

This spiritual side of living and loving should be the objective not only of those who have come adrift in the middle years of life, but of all who reach this period. Life always presents the need for integration between the practical achievements of living, the emotional relationships with others, and the often neglected 'suprapersonal', or the spiritual dimension of living. The first half of life is occupied with growth and development. There is the desire to succeed and the possibility of doing so. There is also the opportunity for forming good personal relationships first of all in the family, and then in other groups and the community at large. These two things demand the greater part of a person's attention. It is in middle age that the desire for something beyond all this often asserts itself. For the middle of life provides the opportunity to look both backwards and forwards, to appreciate what has passed, and to prepare for what is to come. It makes possible a new assessment of the purpose of life, and so a new integration between body, mind and spirit.

There is often great need here for the help of the pastoral counsellor, for this desire for integration may be the outcome of despair at what has been lost in the past, and anxiety at what the future seems to offer. The counsellor has to help the person to turn his despair into hope and his anxiety into faith and this is not easy if the person has little understanding of the inner meaning of religion, or has had unfortunate experiences of it in the past.

The pressures against the middle-aged man or woman seeking to find the spiritual side of life are extremely powerful both from without and within. There is often a feeling of embarrassed confusion at discussing anything to do with religion with another person. This is connected probably with the fact that in their young days it was not regarded as suitable to discuss spiritual things, or they connected such matters with disagreeable incidents at home, at school or in adolescence. But more important is the fact of being so accustomed to only the practical and impersonal sides of life that it becomes almost impossible to contact the spiritual. The bustle, noise, togetherness, restless activity and greed to possess have for so long shut out these attributes that it becomes very difficult to reinstate them. The stillness, silence, solitude and timelessness, which are among the requisites for discovering this life, are difficult to find.

Unfortunately much of so-called religion has little to do with the life of the spirit, and it is this which is so much needed at this period of life. The pastoral counsellor is well advised not to begin with religion, particularly in the case of those for whom it has lost its spiritual meaning and intensity. It can often first be resuscitated through something of beauty in music, the arts, poetry or something which seems to speak of the authenticity of the supernatural and makes a person wonder. People who are able to catch a sight of spiritual reality in this way may find later that they return to the religion of their early life, and find in it an entirely new meaning. They may also find that this supplies the power to help them meet the difficulties which this period of their life presents.

COUNSELLING THE ELDERLY

In biological terms the course of human life begins at birth and ends in decay. Between these two extremes lie the periods of growth, of procreation and of productivity. Looking more closely at these periods it is possible to see that certain processes of decline are already developing during the period of biological growth, and that conversely during the period of biological decline certain component systems continue to develop. Different stages of human achievement can be indicated, each with its own particular characteristics. The first reaches its peak in youth when the achievements are reached in spheres involving physical attributes such as strength and speed. The second is in middle age when a state of maturity and self-confidence has been reached and when the successful have attained the height of their profession or career. The third is in old age when mental attributes such as experience and systematic thinking are the crucial factors and when wisdom has been learnt. The elderly have therefore much to bestow on life if they are capable of doing so and permitted to make their unique contribution.

But there are other circumstances which have to be taken into account. In the first place illness will affect any existing psychic condition. This is, of course, true of all stages of life, but it is especially true of old age, when illnesses are more frequent and physical debilities are unavoidable. Secondly, the general health of old people is influenced by their external circumstances. The way in which a person grows old is determined in no small measure by the way in which he is cared for by his family or by the particular circle in which he is living. What matters is that he should be living in the right kind of environment, with people who are prepared to concern themselves with him, where he feels safe and where he is able to interest himself either in some other person or in some project.

The extent to which the various faculties of the ageing and the aged continue to function efficiently will depend on whether the mind is able to assert its supremacy over the physical disabilities. Old age is capable of positive organisation only if the mental powers of the individual concerned remain sufficiently alert. The last phase of life can either take the form of a synthesis, or it will be a period of disintegration and decay. At the one extreme is the old person who has retained his mental and also his physical health into extreme old age. The mental gifts, the experience acquired by work and integrated with good sense and the overall view which he has gained go to make up the wisdom of such an old person. Here old age has found its fulfilment. At the other extreme the mental curve has followed the biological curve and may even have sunk beneath it. The personality, drained of its mental powers, just goes on existing without really living, and pursues a purely vegetative form of human reality without participating in anything or anybody. Most old people lie somewhere between these extremes.

It is only possible to understand old age if the preceding periods of life with their inner experiences, their various stages of internal and external development and their physical and psychic occurrences are taken into account. The personality of old people is stamped not only by their constitution and heredity but also by their biological and pathological biography and by the internal and external experiences of the whole course of their earlier life. At the same time, however, every human life is unique and unrepeatable. Thus it is that individual character traits become more and more pronounced in old age, and the older a person becomes the more individual he gets. No two old people ever pose exactly the same problem and this is what makes counselling the old so very difficult.

In order to understand older people, it is necessary to remember that their sociological situation, their position in the family, and in society at large, undergoes a change. Parents and the older generation have disappeared from the scene and friends and contemporaries begin to die. Thus a person tends to lose the security which his personal framework had previously afforded him. People need to feel that they belong somewhere and the majority of people get this sense of belonging from their family and their work. The older a person becomes the more the rising generation will threaten and encroach upon his position and his privileges. He will be gently pushed into a backwater and will be expected to accept this transition without as much as a word of protest or a sign of anger towards the younger people who have pushed him out. Old men and women often find themselves in a situation in which they are required to recognise and even to admire the leadership of those whom they had once known as immature young people.

The reason why loneliness is felt so intensely by old people is that the change of generations is accompanied by a change of cultures and this is particularly pronounced today. Catch phrases, books, fashion and personalities are the outward signs of such cultures, and whilst the old will still respond at the mention of some aspect of their own culture, to the young it will mean almost nothing at all. This is why ancient friendships are often resuscitated and renewed. Friends of youth will often find one another again in old age and such old friendships are maintained against considerable differences of political and religious conviction for they draw their strength from an inner attitude that has been conditioned from a common past.

Retirement is one of the crucial external changes to which people have to adapt themselves when they grow old. The way in which they do this depends very much on the nature of their work, and on their state of health. People engaged on physical work often show signs of fatigue long before retirement and are pleased when that time comes. Others are glad to be relieved of the heavy responsibility. Some are tied to occupations to which they are temperamentally unsuited and so are glad to throw them off. In spite of this, retirement is a critical turning point in life and one to which people find it rather difficult to adapt, and which also gives rise to problems of a particular kind in the ensuing period of life.

It is often the abruptness with which people retire in our society which leads to repercussions on the emotional and mental stability. Retirement changes the habits of a lifetime and the whole course of the day with its alternating rhythm of work and leisure. When a person goes into retirement he is forced to acknowledge that he is old in every sense of the word and that the most important part of his life is over and done with. Now he has entered into the final phase of life. The transition is much easier for those who have some occupation which they can do part-time or for people with an absorbing hobby. Professional women with a home to look after will often have a feeling of relief at being less busy.

From the very beginning of his career a man is obliged to live in two worlds, a working world and a domestic one, and each of these two environments calls for a particular type of attitude and a particular form of behaviour. This double life, which a man lives for several decades, can produce a definite split in his personality, which will be all the more serious the more he tends to identify with his working life at the expense of his real life. Then when he retires he is unable to adjust to the demands of domesticity. Some personalities are particularly badly placed in this respect and suffer intensely on retirement. Similarly retirement may bring out personality defects in people which had previously been camouflaged by their professional activities.

People's reactions to retirement differ according to their character, their mental powers and the extent to which they have inwardly prepared themselves for it. Many feel a sense of relief and freedom, others grow bitter and complain about the injustice of the world and the ingratitude of their fellows. Many suffer from a sense of emptiness and fall victim to deadly boredom. Often those suffering from the negative effects are unable to rid themselves of them, and then these pent-up forces may show themselves in disturbances of the vegetative nervous system. It is not uncommon for genuine physical illness to emerge. The symptoms of such illness will, of course, have been present before retirement, but will now come to the fore and take over. Retirement may lead, in some, to a rapid decline which ends only in death.

It is for this reason that attempts are made today to prepare people for retirement by discussing its problems with them several years before it actually takes place, and by suggesting how it may be possible to find some interesting and suitable substitute occupation. Counsellors who are engaged in this form of helping others need to have a very shrewd knowledge of human personality and be able to direct a person along the lines which are likely to be of satisfaction to him and to make his retirement a pleasurable experience. They also need to be aware of possible personality clashes between husband and wife when the husband retires. Marriage crises are more frequent at this late age than would be expected, for a man and wife may now be thrown together all day long – a fact that may not have happened since their honeymoon. Retirement may reveal the weakness of the bonds between them and lead to much unhappiness. On the other hand, it can lead to a more exalted and more intimate relationship if both partners are fundamentally capable of such affinity.

Problems of finance and prestige will also arise with retirement for few manage to maintain the level of their income and even fewer to keep the position of authority and respect which they had when they were at work. The greater expectation of life which is now possible and the threats of devaluation and inflation cause very real monetary worries and difficulties for those on a small pension, while those who had previously occupied high positions do not necessarily ask for gratitude but they do at least expect to be still consulted on particular issues of which they have expert knowledge.

An old person's need for security is not restricted to financial and economic considerations alone. He wants to feel secure in every department of life. He wants continuity in his personal relationships and in his physical environment. This will undoubtedly bring difficulties, for as activities outside the home have to be curtailed or given up through some fall, severe illness or other physical condition, his way of life has to be changed. He may be faced with blindness, or with deafness or with loss of memory, and this may mean a move from a flat or room which he has occupied for some time and come to regard as his anchor in life. Or his relatives may find themselves no longer able to keep him with them and a move means not only loss of them but of his other friends as well. Counselling can be very difficult in these cases for the facts of the situation may be obvious, and yet the person be quite unwilling to accept them. Only patient understanding and explanation is likely to lead to a change in attitude, and very rarely will such loss of independence be fully accepted.

Old people also need to feel that they are safely enclosed in a warm and loving circle, and to feel at home in the broadest sense of the word. They seek compensations for the deprivations which old age inevitably imposes. They would consider a friendly environment to be one in which people were interested not only in their present lives but also in their past. Their assessment of themselves is primarily concerned with their past and with the beauty and pleasure of the experiences which they once enjoyed. Thus, if a counsellor is to reach an old person's heart his interest will have to be extended to the past life of the old person as well as to the present. This will not be entirely a waste of time, for much can be gleaned about the person from the sorts of things which he remembers.

Many old people are depressed because they feel that they have no longer any purpose in life. They would like to feel that in their environment and in their circle, no matter how small and insignificant it may be, they still count for something. This is particularly so when debilities and deprivations make a person feel inferior and useless. Often it takes very little to give an old person the feeling that he is still able to contribute to the lives of other people and to participate in their activities. Casual suggestions in line with his known interests may help in this way. There are many tasks for which old people are better equipped than those of younger years, particularly those which demand a sense of responsibility and precision rather than productivity or flexibility. Thus, there is a great need for finding out what old people are still able to do rather than listing the things which they cannot do.

On the other hand, old age may be a time of great opportunity, for it is a period when there is more leisure and more solitude. There is time to listen, to think, to consider and perhaps to read books which required too much effort when the only available time was the end of the day. With the knowledge that death is not so far away, it is often a time of taking stock. The majority of old people speak about such matters very little, and yet they may be the basis of their thoughts for much of their waking hours, and many of their sleepless ones as well.

The counsellor's task will be to help such people in a positive manner. The one who is much alone will need to find a self worth living with; that is his real self. If he has sought this earlier in life it will not be difficult to help him to continue in his search; and for the spiritually minded person this time of life will be one of great joy and peace at the thought that he is approaching the fulfilment of all that he believes.

There can also be much negative retrospection. Those who

indulge in this kind of introspection are not necessarily troubled by any moral failings to which they may have been subject in the past, but rather by their failure or inability to exhaust all available sources of pleasure or success. They remember, with annoyance, every occasion which might have afforded them these things and which they allowed to slip by without taking advantage of them. Their reaction is anger and disappointment, and the wise counsellor can do little more than listen, sum up for them all that has been said, and integrate into meaningful relationships the events of the person's lifetime in the perspective of the present.

But there may be retrospection of a more neurotic nature. Old people may consider the past with feelings of guilt and apprehension, and this may not only discomfort them, but disturb their emotional stability. All the harm that a person has done to his fellows and all the wilful mistakes which he has made in the course of his life can rebound with great force upon his head. Counselling may then become an examination of all that stands between the soul and God, with perhaps the need for confession and forgiveness before such things can be removed and the sense of guilt obliterated. It may then lead to great spiritual advance with the comfort and joy which accompanies this. On the other hand, there may be the need for the help of a psychiatrist, for it is not always the past as it actually happened which will make a person feel retrospectively guilty. The crucial factors are the depth and the differentiation of the experiences of which the person is capable, and the extent to which these have led to much brooding and feelings of guilt. In one way or another such problems have to be integrated, and when the unconscious is deeply involved it is beyond the scope of counselling.

In order to advance towards maturity, the experiences which a person has undergone must be consciously integrated. It is not so much the amount and variety of experiences that a person passes through, as their conscious integration and reflection which can stimulate, instruct and encourage a man. Every loss and every sorrow can become a source of new strength and new knowledge. Old age is then accepted as a trial that has to be overcome, and as a necessary stage of inner development, and can then be worked upon at a conscious level. In this way a person accepts his fate, both as it is in the present, and as it will be when the future has added its quota. Without the negative experiences, accidents and acts of failure he simply could not have become the person that he is. But he does not spend time on idle conjecture as to how these things might have been if he had not done this or that, but he acquires an overall view of his entire life and all the contradictions inherent in it. He has to stand back and look at himself from a distance, and then use the knowledge that he has gained to anticipate the future and to strengthen his resources against whatever may be in store. He is then well on the way to the goal of maturity.

The time comes when some of the restrictions of old age begin to accumulate. Activities outside the home have to be curtailed or given up and the loss of personal independence may become a very grave deprivation. The bedridden and the helpless are not only a burden to themselves, but they are often worried at being a burden to others because they need so much attention and nursing care. The instinctive reaction is to resent restriction and to indulge in self pity, to envy the unfettered and to question and to rebel. Yet the way to meet these things and to overcome them is to accept them and make friends of them. Fortunately, with the decline in physical powers, the soul often reveals new abilities. These begin to develop when the physical body which encompasses them begins to fail. When a person is still fully active, and achievement is the main concern of life, the functions which provide for this achievement tend to be promoted more than other functions. But when death approaches and the vital forces are sapped, then the deep-rooted aspects of the inner life may begin to emerge and to take over from the more superficial and functional aspects. This kind of development is possible only to the person who accepts what life offers him, and is able to greet old age and its discomforts with some pleasure. In this last phase of life a person has to set his house in order, consider how best to come to terms with his disabilities, and what attitudes to adopt to his fellow men and the members both of his immediate environment and of society in general. In all this the understanding and patient counsellor plays a helpful but unobtrusive part, doing much by his presence and support rather than by any active guidance.

Man's attitude to death and the realisation that life must come to an end varies enormously from one person to another. To some extent this depends upon the ability to face up to the unexpected, and to the undesired. A person who has fully lived his life will have acquired a great power of resistance in the course of years, and have a greater degree of invulnerability because as he grows older he will have learnt to master the anticipation of events, to deal with happenings as they come, and to regard the future, whatever it may offer, as well within his powers of acceptance.

This awareness of death as something which is a part of our human reality probably comes to most people about the middle of life. Often it will be prompted by some external factor, such as an illness, an accident, the apparent signs of old age, or the loss of a relative or near friend. It may induce a wide variety of reactions, depending upon the temperament, the attitude to life of the person concerned, and the sorts of experiences he has undergone in his life which may have turned him into a hopeful or a pessimistic sort of person.

At the one extreme there is the feeling that death is a brutal intrusion undertaken by some external force or a fate which suddenly descends at some specific moment of time. At the other extreme is the attitude that death is immanent in life and belongs to life, and without death life cannot be rounded off into an entity. It belongs to life as a fated and entirely logical sequence. In this case a person is not only invulnerably prepared for death, but sometimes he even longs for it. Most people fall somewhere between these two extremes, and it behoves the counsellor to judge just where and to help him accordingly.

Counselling those who are approaching death can be a most intimate and difficult task. The priest has the comfort of the sacraments to offer, and for those who understand and appreciate these things, they can be an immense boon. Some too, feel that the sacraments possess a supernatural power and this helps them through one of the most difficult periods of life. But the counsellor has to try to understand a person's attitude to death, and the place where he most needs support and this may not necessarily be of a religious nature. Quite often it will be the active presence of another human being to help the person to meet the utter loneliness which death brings. Here, perhaps more than in any other form of counselling, it is a sustaining relationship which is needed, and this can be brought about in a manifold manner of ways. Deep understanding and perceptiveness are the counsellor's most valued requisites.

The great need in our society is to accept death as a part of life, rather than to cover it up and pretend that it barely exists. The appropriate attitude is to face its challenge and counselling, perhaps in groups, could do much to help older people to reach this state of mind and be ready to accept it when it comes. Much of the fear of death lies in the fact that people do not talk about it and so have little idea as to how others feel. If these feelings could be expressed, then a person would be able to understand how someone else was coping with them, and comfort would be found in companionship.

VIII. Counselling and Healing

Health implies harmony or wholeness within the personality, a harmony of body, mind and spirit, of the conscious and the unconscious. It involves the integration of all these into an individual or an undivided person who meets the ups and downs of life with equanimity and whose balance when upset returns fairly easily to a position of equilibrium. It also involves satisfactory interpersonal relationships both with other people and with God, so that the person is able to enjoy the company of others and to be himself enjoyed. Hence it is harmony within oneself and within the I-Thou relationship.

The function of healing is to bring this about, and in this sense it means not only the recovery of health when this is lost, but the prevention of ill-health and the promotion of good health. It is generally agreed that health and healing are inseparable from life itself and that they come through a power given and constantly replenished with life. Healing is in general a rational, law-abiding process, intimately related to the laws of life and growth. Healthy life, growth and reproduction depend upon human co-operation with these laws, but the power of healing lies beyond the power of man. All that man can do is to seek to co-operate with this inner healing power.

He is able to provide this co-operation both on the medical and the spiritual level. Medical science can do this by using its knowledge about surgery, medicine and sometimes of interpersonal relationships to help the individual who is sick in mind or body. It can also attempt to remove the possible hindrances to health and healing. Religion can do similar things on the spiritual level. It can constantly renew the inner resources of faith, hope and love so that a person is enabled to overcome the spiritual hindrances to health and live in an atmosphere of peace and joy. Spiritual help not only complements medical attention, but it goes beyond it by reaching out to the creative power of God.

There are wide divergences as to the relative importance of these two aspects of healing. At one extreme there are the people who believe that the real ministry of healing has now been taken over almost completely by medical science in the form of medical knowledge, surgery, psychiatry and all their associated services. They accept with gratitude the services of pastors as hospital chaplains and visitors, the provision and administrations of hospitals and homes by the churches, and the private ministry to the sick. But they do not generally regard these services as playing any essential part in the actual work of healing. They regard them as incidental to the main task of healing which is in the hands of the doctors, nurses and the medical social workers.

At the other extreme is spiritual healing, which is the practice of healing by spiritual means by getting at men's ailments through their spirits rather than through their minds or their bodies. Some of the agencies of spiritual healing are to be found within the Christian church and most denominations have special organisations for this purpose, although they do not usually isolate spiritual healing but accept some degree of medical and psychiatric help as well. But far more of such agencies are outside the church. Some are sheer charlatanry but others, though connected with beliefs that the church cannot accept, are practised successfully and many of their practitioners are selfless, devoted and untiring people.

This dichotomy between the medical and spiritual aspects of healing is largely the result of historical causes. Although in primitive times healing was indistinguishable from religion, a distinction very soon developed and health became regarded as the greatest good and disease as a curse which removed man from the place of perfection. There was a love for the beautiful and the successful and for those who were undoubtedly in conformity with the cosmos, but no love for the crippled and the elderly nor was anything done to try to heal them or to improve their lot in life. Christianity at first stressed the unity of body, soul and spirit and the need for wholeness of the personality. But this idea was gradually lost and illness became related to sin. Modern scientific medicine, as would be expected, regarded such an idea as untenable, and so medicine has developed as a natural science, open to rational thinking, but taking little cognisance of the irrational dimensions of life. It has become open to experimentation and investigation, but not to anything which might savour of the supernatural.

It is now becoming more generally realised however that both the medical and the spiritual aspects of healing are necessary. On the one hand, the most efficient and devoted medical care may leave a person reasonably healed in body and mind, but still sick in his soul and therefore incompletely healed. On the other hand, religion cannot deal effectively with all forms of disease. Spiritual help is needed to reinforce what is being done by other agencies. It is through the co-ordination of both medical and spiritual skills that complete healing is made possible

The church has several ways of dealing with this urgent problem of healing. In the first place there is the traditional, priestly one of using prayer and the sacramental methods of laying on of hands and of anointing with oil. While there is a strong desire for healing, there is no attempt to dwell on the hope of any particular result, but simply on the love and power of God, with the fullest acceptance of any or no apparent change in the body or mind. Such healing is an attempt to bring the soul of the sick person into direct communion with the creative, redemptive and healing power of God. It is healing at and from the very centre of the personality and so is distinct from any other kinds of healing efforts, medical, surgical or psychiatric, though it usually works in co-operation with these other kinds of healing.

A less familiar, though very important kind of healing is that which can be offered by the Christian congregation. The loving concern of others is a great incentive to recovery from sickness and a congregation can practise its healing ministry by praying for the sick, by visiting them in hospital or at home, and by accepting persons, whether sick in body or in mind, as part of themselves. Some illnesses such as alcoholism, drug addiction and epilepsy can well be approached on a group basis, and the congregation can take part in this by providing facilities and support to those who suffer in this way. Similarly, members of a congregation can help those in convalescence after illness by taking them into their own homes for a short time, or by helping to maintain homes and hostels where such people can stay until they are ready to face the stresses and strains of ordinary life.

Pastoral counselling is a very important part of healing, for not only is it a means towards healing in its own right, but it also should form part of all the priestly forms of healing as well as being an ancillary to the efforts which are made by Christian congregations to welcome those who are in need of help into their midst. Pastoral counselling is particularly needed for sick people who find personal relationships difficult and this is often accentuated in hospital surroundings. It is even more essential where persons are suffering on account of some broken or marred relationship which may consciously or unconsciously be affecting their recovery. Similarly the person who finds the way to healing through a healing service should be able to have the personal counselling which is vital for the continuance of the process, and the person who finds help in the fellowship of a Christian congregation should have the opportunity for deeper and longer individual therapy.

COUNSELLING THE SICK

Visiting the sick and counselling the sick are not always synonymous, for some of those who are ill will be fully able to deal with their own problems and resent any efforts at help. But sick-visiting is a unique opportunity for helping those who would like some help but might otherwise be diffident about coming for counselling. It is also a time when people realise that they are not quite so independent as they had imagined they were. Sickness is a sign that well-being has been threatened or endangered and the basic emotional response is one of fear, a fear of what may happen to oneself, to one's family and often of death itself. The reaction to fear is either to fight it or to flee, and so this reaction may take the form of a bald denunciation of God or whatever is thought to have caused the situation to arise in a person who is normally temperate in his attitudes. Or, on the other hand, it may lead to a withdrawal into self and a turning away from anyone who may be trying to help. A counsellor has to be prepared for such attitudes and to be able to meet them.

The counsellor will find it very difficult to enter into the feelings of the sick unless he himself has come to terms with the problems of pain, suffering, sickness and of death. In spite of all the research and deep searchings which have been made into these problems, they still remain an impenetrable and overwhelming mystery. To some, disease and death are regarded as the symbols of the disorder that is found in the world as the result of the use of man's freewill. They were not intended as part of creation, but have resulted from the freedom of choice which was given to man. Thus there is a link between death, disease and sin, but it is one of a general connection, intelligible only in the perspective of human interdependence, and not of a strict connection between a particular sin and a particular illness or death – at least this is very rarely the case. Sickness appears to be consequential rather than punitive, and often vicarious and unmerited.

True healing is regarded by the Christian as a restoration of the wholeness of the personality and as a reconciliation with men and with God. Death itself can also be seen in this way, and as part of this process. For death can lead to a larger and fuller part of the unbroken life which man is intended to have with his fellow men and with God.

But to the person who is not a Christian such ideas are quite unintelligible and often most offensive. It is generally a waste of time and even harmful on occasions to present the Christian approach in terms such as these to those who are non-church-goers and even to some who do go to church. The passport of the Christian counsellor is largely in terms of his personal devotion and understanding of relationships, and these are the means whereby he can overcome the defence mechanisms of the sick person and can help him to gain some insight into himself and to the problems of pain and of suffering.

Counselling the sick requires a modification of the usual counselling techniques, due partly to the setting in which such counselling takes place, and partly to the fact that the person may not be well enough to take an active part. Whether the counselling takes place in the home or in hospital it is not always entirely at the will of the person himself. The success of a first contact will depend very much upon whether the visit has been made at the request of the person who is ill, or of his relatives, or on the counsellor's own initiative. In the latter cases it may take some time before confidence is established with the counsellor. When a sick person does not desire to talk, more harm than good arises from staying. A contact has been made and this can be followed up later on if the person wishes it.

The first few moments at the bedside are usually the crucial ones. The sick person may not know what to do with the counsellor and may feel embarrassed and shy. It is usually up to the counsellor to begin talking and if he is not already known to the sick person he can best do so by saying who he is, what his responsibilities are and, if the person is in hospital, what he can do to help the person while he is there. This explanation needs to be centred on the patient rather than the counsellor and to suggest that the purpose of their meeting is to enable the person to use his own resources to combat his illness. There is often the temptation, when there are awkward pauses, to discuss the trivialities of life, and then it may be very difficult to pass on to anything else. Sick people are usually very willing to talk about deeper things, but very shy to start, and so will politely enter into long conversations about the weather and similar topics.

Sickness usually brings a person up against the realities of life, and this may be the first time that he has been able to stop and think. It may give him an opportunity to brood over things that have lain submerged in his subconscious, of talking them over with another person, and of perhaps confessing something that has been latently troubling him for a long time. The main job of the counsellor, as is always the case, is to listen and to understand. If the sick person has an opportunity of saying what he really feels he will get to know himself better and may discover what are the real problems that he has to face and perhaps see the meaning of his sickness. Conversation of this nature is by no means easy, though it can often be encouraged by the counsellor himself telling of a personal experience of a similar type. Once the bond of friendship is established and the sick person feels that he is no longer alone then it is possible for things of importance to come up. Conversation of this type is not merely a relief; it is often the first step in the healing process.

A hospital setting introduces certain complications, since the authoritarian attitude of medicine does not fit in well with the permissive nature of counselling. The aim must be to restore a sense of self-responsibility to the patient. The counsellor, and in this case it is often the hospital chaplain, has to divorce himself from the authoritative aspect of the setting of which he is an integral part, and at the same time help the patient to accept and follow the prescribed régime. With regard to the patient, the counsellor has to accept the reaction to authority and allow for his free expression of hostility to those who exercise this authority and to hospital routine in general. He may also have to impart to the doctor his conviction of the patient's right to participate actively in decisions which may affect his future. In this way the patient can be assured that he has importance and is a self-directing person whose right to free choice is accepted and recognised. With suitable counselling, he can then be able more easily to accept the necessary course of treatment, to which he might otherwise have been resistant.

The problems of the sick vary with the individual patient, with the different stages of his illness, and at the different points of his hospital experience. When he is first ill and needs to go into hospital he is faced with one set of problems. The problems of the person who feels that he is not getting better are quite different from those of the person who is getting well, and the permanently incapacitated person has another set of problems.

Not only does the counsellor have to understand the meaning of illness to people in general, but he has to understand the meaning of this particular illness to this particular person. A careful appraisal of the effect of the illness and the possible residual disability on the everyday life of the person needs to be considered if this is by any means possible, for it can affect the whole direction of the counselling. Even more important is this particular person's reaction to illness, which is largely determined by his personality and his life experiences before he became ill. The counsellor has to bear in mind that a sick person is particularly susceptible to strains, stresses, and conflicts. The ways in which he has coped with these in normal life will tend to determine how he reacts when he is sick. But his reactions under sickness are often greatly exaggerated, and so he may become over-complimentary, dominating, and fault-finding, inclined to misrepresent what is said, or not to hear or understand it.

The sudden change in his usual way of functioning, the

separation from accustomed surroundings and everyday associations, the need to accept a milieu which is strange and therefore frightening, and to submit himself to procedures which are alien and often uncomfortable, sometimes painful, threaten to disturb the sick person. He fears these new forces which interfere with his role as an independent, self-sufficient and self-directing member of the community, and these fears are often reinforced by the reality of his situation. The counsellor has to maintain at all times an appreciation of him as an individual, and a respect for his rights to function as a human being, regardless of the stage of his illness and the state of the incapacity it produces. It is often easier to achieve this if the counsellor is working as a member of a team in a hospital, for then he can call upon other members to contribute their own specific knowledge to help to sustain the patient.

Helplessness, bewilderment and insecurity are the inevitable feelings of the sick and the counsellor needs to counteract these by reinforcing his feelings of worth and importance. These feelings are relieved, not by superficial or false assurances, but through reliable and authoritative answers to the questions which trouble the sick person. The counsellor cannot give answers, but he can create the atmosphere in which these can be given and prepare the person for what may be coming. The patient has to be helped at all times to accept the reality of the situation, so that he neither exaggerates the seriousness of his illness, nor minimises its impact on the adjustments he will be compelled to make.

The reactions of sick people to illness are variable, and the counsellor needs to be aware of this, and to adjust his methods accordingly. Usually the reactions are those which would occur under similar states of anxiety in ordinary life, though they may tend to be exaggerated. Sometimes the dependence of sickness is welcomed when it satisfies a profound suppressed need. At other times it may arouse deep conflicts of which the person has so far been unaware. Or it may even lead to the feeling of complete obliteration of the person as an individual and so to the inability to care. The experienced counsellor should be able to detect these reactions and take account of them in his counselling.

The time factor plays an important part in counselling the sick, for rarely is it possible to arrange a series of visits, nor to be sure that a particular visit is undisturbed. Much may have to be crammed into a very short space of time, and this may mean that the person does not entirely choose the pace which the counselling takes. On the other hand, there is often the urge on the part of the counsellor to say more than he would normally say and this probably arises because he fails to realise that counselling the sick cannot be as complete as ordinary counselling. He can usually only start a process which may be added to, when the person returns home, by the general practitioner, the social worker or the local clergyman or minister. The rule for keeping to the pace of the person being counselled holds as much for the sick person as it does for the well, and experience frequently proves that a very small step forward is likely to lead to more lasting results than the completion of some preconceived plan.

Counselling the sick will often mean helping a person to die. The attitude of faith with which the counsellor speaks about death is of the most vital importance. If the counsellor is himself filled with the certainty of life after death, so that he can testify quite naturally to its reality, he will find it far easier to talk to the dying. For he can then speak more of eternal life as a natural stage of development, and death as the beginning of a far deeper and fuller life than has been led so far. If he is really convinced of this in the depths of his being, this knowledge will convey itself to the person, even if the words themselves may be few and formal and the sick person unable to fully understand them. Pastoral counselling has, at this stage, passed beyond the limits of helping a person to help himself. It has become supportive, and the means whereby the person is helped to face his deepest fears and anxieties, which are always connected, consciously or unconsciously, with death.

The family of the deceased person may also stand in need of counselling, and, in fact, the good counsellor will already be in touch with its members so that he knows them reasonably intimately when they require reassurance and consolation. Anxiety about the sick person when he is ill will be replaced by grief if he dies. Grief has an important part to play in healing for it is not only concerned with what has happened to the person who has died, but with what is likely to happen to the bereaved. Real grief is intended to involve emancipation from bondage to the deceased, a readjustment to the environment in which the deceased is missing, and the formation of a new set of relationships. Mourning patterns for primitive tribes bore these needs in mind, but our modern approach with its emphasis on the suppression of grief often fails to offer the psychological help which is needed at this time. Grief is an emotion and like all emotions involves physical changes which can be extremely sharp. It is likely to bring back emotions which accompanied previous experiences and also to release emotions which had been suppressed. Hence for a time the personality of the bereaved person may seem to change, and guilt feelings may be present which are as often based on fantasy as they are on fact.

The immediate need of the bereaved person is support to help him to pass through the period of shock. It is often thought that when the coming of death has been known for some time less support is required when it actually arrives. Shock occurs at death, whether or not it has been anticipated, and it is the ability of the person to bear the shock which is the first concern of the counsellor. After a short time it is necessary to actualise the loss and this can be done by talking about the person in as normal and interesting a manner as possible, and to discuss the place which will have to be filled in the family. Then the time has arrived to admit sorrow and to encourage the expression of grief. Since our culture has little place for this, grief is often converted into hostility. Therefore this hostility needs recognition and verbalisation. Some will need the help of a counsellor more than others in dealing with grief, and this will depend very much on their own understanding of themselves and on the help which they receive from others in the community.

It is therefore very necessary that the community should recognise its responsibility in this respect. It is only lately that group support has been actively used to help the bereaved, for until recently it was not realised that the period of adjustment was so long and so difficult. Those who continued to mourn were thought to be lacking in character rather than using their mourning as a means of adapting themselves to normal living. The Cruse Clubs for widows, which have been started in Richmond and other urban centres are an example of group therapy for the bereaved. The members are all newly widowed, and meet one another to discuss their mutual problems and to gain support from others who are facing similar situations. By talking together they are enabled to release many feelings which might otherwise have been suppressed, and they can also discuss the practical problems which loom so large in the future of all those who have now to live on their own.

Death is not the only time when the counsellor will become involved with the family of the sick person he is helping. He will often have to help the family accept the person on discharge from hospital, and this may mean interpreting the attitude of the patient to the family. Sickness may have temporarily altered his ability to live a normal life, or it may have made him fearful of a further onset of illness and so difficult to live with. Counselling on these problems should begin while the person is still in hospital, not only to make the person aware of difficulties when he returns home, but to help the other members of his family to understand him. Practical details, such as living arrangements, work adjustment, and medical follow-up will often supplement this.

Sometimes the sick person has to face permanent disability or chronic sickness. There is then a special need for counselling. Reactions to such a situation are variable. Sometimes depression sets in coupled with gloomy rumination, or anger which expresses itself in resentment or hostility. There may be an inner struggle between denial and acceptance, or between dependence and autonomy. The counsellor has to accompany such a person through his period of anguish, depression or rage and stand at his side in the struggle with doubts and confusion. He has to work with him towards a new inner balance which will involve a realistic acceptance and accommodation of what the future will hold for him. It means both a meeting between two persons and an encounter between two worlds. The counsellor has to be able to comprehend the world in which the person is now forced to live, with all its limitations and seeming degradations and by forming a good relationship with him help him to accept them and adapt himself to them.

If a child becomes handicapped or chronically sick he usually thinks he will get well, and so the problem is one of a gradual physical adjustment to his new condition. But the adolescent, for instance one who is injured in a car accident, may find things far more difficult, for he is able to visualise the future and the extent of his loss. Such a person has a special need for a counsellor who will give him continuous support and help him to know that what he feels, thinks and says is still important. When the counsellor works in close contact with the doctor, the social worker and any others who are helping as well, there is likely to be more progress.

The parents of a handicapped or disabled child are often in greater need of help than the child itself. They have probably looked forward to its birth, and when it is born handicapped their plans and dreams are destroyed, and their conscious and unconscious needs frustrated. They feel shocked, disappointed, and even guilty. Much of this can be traced to our cultural emphasis on normality, and to the constant comparison which is made with neighbours. The disability comes as an affront to the family standing in the community, and where there are brothers and sisters the relationships with the handicapped child may become complex and difficult. Reactions will be varied, depending on the general atmosphere or love of the family, the extent and severity of the handicap, the age of the handicapped child and of the other children. There may be the fear that they will become the same, or they will resent the extra care and protection which is lavished on the handicapped child.

In situations like this there is a great need for pastoral counselling to help the parents accept the full nature of the child's handicap so that they may reach an emotional equilibrium. Time spent with frightened and distraught parents, recognising their plight and giving them some support with their burdens, will help a great deal to soften the blow and prepare the way for a realistic and constructive adjustment to the handicap. It may take many hours of patient listening and the working through of adverse feelings before a state of acceptance can be reached, and only then is it possible to begin to plan for the future.

Not only is the pastor needed in these circumstances, but the church congregation is needed as well. It can help in the first place by warmly taking the parents into their midst, by encouraging them to talk about their problems, and by giving them support and help when this is needed. One of the main difficulties of anyone caring for the handicapped is the complete lack of leisure, and the members of a congregation can help to make some free time possible. Similarly a congregation can accept the adult disabled person, and make it easier for him to participate in the ordinary life of the community. The great need for the handicapped person is to be able to forget his disability and to look upon himself as an ordinary person.

THE MENTALLY ILL

The mentally ill as well as the physically ill can often be helped by counselling. The only ones for whom counselling help is useless are those whose whole personality has been affected. Such people are not aware that they need help and so they are unable to co-operate in any way with the counsellor. But they can be supported by friendliness, warmth and understanding, and they are often most grateful for it. Those for whom counselling can be of great use are people suffering from the neuroses for, with such people, only part of the personality is affected and they are usually desperately anxious to become themselves again. But it is necessary to have a very good knowledge of counselling processes before attempting to help a person with neurotic tendencies.

It is generally agreed that the basis of neurosis is conflict. Yet it is not neurotic to have conflicts. All living involves choice. In a stable and tradition-bound society choices are limited so that the possible range of individual conflicts is narrow. But, in a society such as ours today, with change more rapid than it has ever been before, there are highly contradictory values and divergent ways of living with the result that the choices an individual has to make are manifold and difficult. For example, a person may have to choose whether to conform to the expectations of the community or to be a dissenting individual. He can be gregarious or he can keep himself to himself. He can court success or he can despise it. He can bring up his children with strict discipline or he can allow them to grow up as they like. He can believe in different moral standards for men and women, or he can regard them as the same for both sexes. He can foster racial discrimination or take the stand that human values are independent of the colour of the skin or facial expression. These and many others are issues which have to be faced today.

Most people get by without suffering deep conflicts because they manage without taking definite sides. They are constantly making compromises without being aware of doing so, and becoming involved in contradictions without knowing it. Some people, however, recognise these contradictory issues and are able to deal with them. They are aware of what their feelings and wishes are, and they develop their own set of values. They are willing and able to make some definite stand on an issue and they can take the risk of making the wrong decision and of bearing the consequences without putting the blame on to others. To be able to experience conflicts knowingly is a very valuable asset, but it is possible to help people to do this. Knowledge should enable a person to live with a greater awareness of himself and to develop his convictions. A realisation of the significance of the factors involved in choice should give a person ideals for which to strive and so lead to a direction for his life. Much of the work of the pastoral counsellor in helping those who come to him with conflicts is involved in encouraging this.

For the neurotic, however, the difficulties always inherent in recognising and resolving a conflict are greatly increased. There are, of course, degrees of being neurotic, but for the more severely neurotic person the factors involved are absolutely incompatible. Not only this but the whole conflict frequently remains unconscious and only comes to the surface occasionally in the form of sudden anger or rage. The emotional factors involved may be rationalised into such things as an injustice or a slight, and the decision to move in one direction or another may be entirely compulsive.

The main difference between the normal and neurotic conflict lies fundamentally in the fact that the disparity in conflict issues is much less great for the normal. Even though a normal person may be unaware of his conflict, he can recognise it with comparatively little help, while the essential tendencies of a neurotic conflict are deeply repressed and can be unearthed only against great resistance. Normal conflict is concerned with actual choice between two possibilities, both of which the person finds really desirable, or between two convictions, both of which he really values. It is therefore possible for him to arrive at a feasible decision, even though it may be very difficult for him and require a renunciation of some kind. On the other hand, the neurotic is not free to choose. He is driven by equally compelling forces in opposite directions, neither of which he wants to follow.

To detect neurotic conflicts is by no means easy, partly because they are unconscious, but even more because the neurotic goes to great lengths to deny their existence. Their presence, however, is indicated by two factors. The first of these is symptoms. Unresolved conflicts can lead to a variety of states, including anxiety, depression, indecision, inertia and detachment or to some form of anti-social behaviour such as stealing. The second factor is inconsistency. A person strongly supports a particular mode of action but does just the opposite himself, or he longs for something which he takes no steps to obtain. These symptoms and inconsistencies are to be found to some extent in most of us, but when they are marked they serve to point to a basic conflict which is the dynamic centre from which the neuroses emanate.

The neurotic will put an amazing amount of energy and intelligence into trying to do away with his conflicts. He may repress certain aspects of his personality and bring their opposites to the fore, hoping that in this way he will improve his relations with other people. Or he may put a distance between himself and his fellows so that the conflicts are put out of operation. He may move away from himself by creating in place of himself an idealised image in which the conflicting parts are so transfigured that they no longer appear as conflicts but as various aspects of a rich personality. Or he may externalise conflicts which are going on within himself by attributing them to other people. He will feel someone else is angry with him, while he is really angry with himself. These and many other ways of dealing with conflicts are found in varying degrees in most neurotic conditions.

A first consequence of these unresolved conflicts is fear. The neurotic finds that as time passes the basic conflict remains but he also gets involved in many new conflicts. So he does his best to take defensive positions in each case. Hence the intense fear that something will jeopardise these positions which he has taken with such trouble. It may be a fear of change, of insanity, of disregard, of humiliation, of ridicule or of many other things but whatever form it takes, it stands in the way of his need to face himself.

A second is impoverishment of personality. Living with unresolved conflicts involves an enormous waste of human energies, occasioned not only by the conflicts themselves, but by all the devious attempts to remove them. It may also involve a split in matters of a moral nature, that is in moral principles and all the feelings, attitudes, and behaviour that bear upon relations with others and affect a person's own development. It leads to a loss of moral wholeheartedness or to an impairment of moral integrity. So, too, the neurotic's attitude towards responsibility may become confused, for as a rule he does not know what he is doing, or why he is doing it, and he has a keen subjective interest in not knowing.

Though a neurotic can be content at times, despite his conflicts, he tends to get himself inextricably entangled. He is securely caught in his conflicts without any apparent possibility of ever getting out. His attempts at solution not only fail, but increasingly alienate him from himself. The eventual result of this is hopelessness with its deepest roots in the despair of ever being wholehearted or undivided again. This is one of the chief hindrances to the cure of the severe neurotic and is the source of the special problems of depression and suicidal tendencies.

Many persons manage to carry on in the grip of neurotic hopelessness. If their capacity to be creative has not been too much damaged they may manage to concentrate upon a field in which they can be productive. They may submerge themselves in a social or religious movement or in the work of some charitable organisation. Others, adapting themselves to their particular frame of life, may cease to question it and merely try to fulfil their obligations. Some will give up all serious or promising pursuits and turn to the periphery of life, and try to snatch from it some sort of enjoyment, finding their interest in a hobby or in short-lived pleasures like good eating, convivial drinking or minor sexual affairs. Or they may drift, deteriorate and let themselves go to pieces, and so, unable to do any consistent work, they take to obsessive drinking, gambling and whoring. Eventually persons without hope may turn destructive but at the same time try to make an attempt at restitution by living vicariously. This could be an explanation of the sadistic tendencies which are common among such people.

If a person is to overcome his neurotic tendencies, he must acquire the capacity to assume responsibility for himself in the sense of feeling himself the active, responsible factor in his life, capable of making decisions and of taking the consequences. This also implies an acceptance of responsibility towards others and a willingness to recognise obligations whether they relate to his children, parents, friends, employees, colleagues, the community or the nation. Closely connected with this is the aim of achieving an inner independence which means establishing his own scale of values and applying it to his actual way of living, instead of adopting the opinions and beliefs of others, or an attitude of defiance towards them. It involves respect for the individuality of others and their rights, and so should lead to real mutuality.

He also needs to acquire within himself an awareness and aliveness of feeling in respect of love or hate, happiness or sadness, fears or desires. But particularly he needs a capacity for love and friendship which draws him into relationships with others and enables him to share their experiences, and to find understanding, joy and satisfaction in being with others. His ultimate goal should be wholeheartedness, a person without pretence, emotionally sincere, able to put himself into his work, his feelings and his beliefs. These are the ideals to strive for, though few such people are likely to come very near to reaching them. But they are the goals which a counsellor should bear in mind when he is trying to help a person with deep conflicts.

The way of resolving conflicts is by changing those conditions within the personality which brought the conflicts about. This is the task of psychotherapy which involves analysing the entire neurotic structure, examining in detail all unconscious efforts at solution that the person has undertaken and their effects upon the personality. It seeks to bring the person to an awareness of the conflicts themselves and how they operate, and to an understanding of the incompatible drives and attitudes that stem from them. Such treatment follows the same lines as ordinary counselling in that it provides an atmosphere of acceptance in which the patient can unburden his feelings progressively and be encouraged and helped to gain a better insight into all the self-deception which he has built up over the years. But deep analytical therapy over a long period is needed if the patient's defences are to be overcome and if he is to become truly aware of his conflicts and overwhelming emotions. The pastoral counsellor is certainly not equipped for this, and would do more harm than good if he were to try.

The pastoral counsellor can, however, work with the psychotherapist. He can offer compassion and understanding until such psychotherapy can take place, and when the person begins to recover he can join with the psychotherapist in helping the person to build up his personality. Between them they may be able to enable the person to adjust himself to society once more, and to come into contact with groups or organisations which will help to bridge over the period between mental illness and the growth of mental health.

While psychotherapy may be needed for the severe neurosis, life itself can prove a very effective therapist in the less severe cases. Experiences of various kinds can be sufficiently telling to bring about personality changes. The inspiring example of a truly great individual, or a common tragedy, may bring the person into closer contact with others who will help to bring him out of his egocentric isolation. He may find such persons so congenial that manipulating them or avoiding them is not necessary, and so be gradually able to take the same attitude to others. Though neither friendships nor religious experiences can be arranged to meet the needs of a particular person, the pastoral counsellor can bring such a person into surroundings where such things are available.

THE LONELY AND INADEQUATE

In addition to those with neurosis, there is a large group of lonely and unhappy people who although perhaps not generally regarded as being mentally ill do nevertheless suffer from some sort of psychological disturbance which causes misery or slightly abnormal behaviour. Hidden psychological disorders often occur in people who are persistently absent from work, who are particularly prone to accidents and who find themselves constantly maladjusted to life. Many of the elderly and of those who have been in prison or in a mental hospital come within this category. So do those who show anti-social or asocial reactions to life, such as the alcoholic, the drug addict, the sexual pervert, and warped and peculiar people like the eccentric recluse, the inveterate miser and the permanent tramp.

Few of these people will be able to cope adequately with the problems of daily living and will constantly be getting into some sort of difficulty. They may hold a job down for a short time and then be dismissed and they will rarely be in command of any situation. They will be very lonely people, and perhaps anxious and depressed as well. It is people like this that the pastoral counsellor will constantly meet, and he will have to decide whether it is merely a friend that is needed, or whether the person requires help through the process of counselling.

A counsellor will offer friendship to all those who come to him, but he will rarely have the time to undertake systematic befriending as well. This is where others, such as the members of a church congregation or of an interested group, can be brought in. A counsellor may pass on a person to be befriended because he feels that although the person is basically able to cope with his problems, he has got them out of proportion or they are being made worse because he has no one with whom to talk them over. He may decide that counselling might be more successful if the person were not entirely alone between interviews, or that there should be someone to whom the person could go at once in any emergency.

Befriending is strictly non-professional and implies an easy relationship on either side, and the sort of sharing which takes place in ordinary friendship. The befriender is asked to be with the person in whatever situation he happens to be in, and at whatever level he is able to accept. It is a very time-consuming job, and may involve having the person home, or accompanying him on the sorts of pursuits which he would normally follow if he had friends of his own. Its whole purpose is to get the person integrated into the community in some way; and it can be most successfully used to help people to become more confident and so to make new contacts on their own or to develop new interests which they can ultimately follow alone. Thus people who are successful at befriending are those who are sympathetic and able to understand the different problems which are likely to be encountered in those they are befriending. They are not necessarily particularly intelligent people, or people with any special form of qualification.

The anxious, the lonely and the depressed are those who are most likely to respond to befriending. Different forms of anxiety call for different responses on the part of the befriender. The person who is anxious because he is suddenly deprived of the support of another person upon whom he had been very much dependent needs some substitute company. The person who feels that he never does the right thing and that he lets down all those who believe in him requires a personal response which will revive his self-esteem. The person who fears some physical affliction needs medical reassurance and should be persuaded to seek it. But he will have to be constantly reminded that the doctor can be trusted, and he needs support when the diagnosis is made. Helping the anxious person is very tiring to the befriender but its importance lies in the fact that incipient anxiety is often the first step in the direction of more serious mental complications.

Certain types of loneliness are particularly helped by befriending, and this is the case when the cause is physical isolation. This is a very real problem especially for the elderly and those who are strange to a place. The person who has survived the death of friends and family has no one left with whom there are any bonds of friendship. Similarly the young person who has come alone to a big city for the first time feels cut off from all those around him and is in desperate need of someone with whom to spend the long hours of leisure. Friendship is usually the answer to this sort of problem.

Another and more complicated form of loneliness arises from social causes. It is an inner experience and results from rapid change when old ways are being rejected and new ways involve some break with the past. It is not only older people who feel this loneliness as they become part of a world they do not understand. Young people are just as bewildered as they grow up and have to find their own ways of adapting themselves. In both cases they are able to control their own affairs and have the ability to do so, but they are unsure of how to do it. The offer of disinterested friendship and support can often help them to adjust themselves.

A more impenetrable type of loneliness is that which arises from a person's inability to enter into emotional commitments, notwithstanding an intense desire to do so. They are lonely although surrounded by family and friends, and there is a partition which seems to seal them off from the advances of others and to prevent them from responding to any overtures. Such a state is usually beyond the scope of befriending, though the acute sense of loneliness and frustration can be made more bearable by the offer of friendship. Its solution lies in intensive counselling and, in extreme cases, psychotherapy.

The homosexual, to a certain extent, suffers a special form of loneliness which has both social and psychological factors. Socially he is regarded as undesirable and this is because our culture favours heterosexual behaviour. Psychologically he is often unable to achieve any of the sexual relationships with the opposite sex which are an important part of satisfactory human relationships. Such people are desperately in need of counselling, but are often very reluctant to ask for it. The counsellor has not only to make the person feel that he accepts him as he is, and understands his problem, but he may also have to suggest a visit to a doctor or a psychiatrist, since the problem of homosexuality is, in general, too complex to be dealt with through counselling alone. Finally it may be necessary to find some group which will admit him into their fellowship, for such people not only suffer from the usual pangs of loneliness, but are prone to sudden panic and depression, and are vulnerable to impulses of suicide. Acceptance and understanding by an ordinary group of people can make all the difference to the homosexual. On the other hand some prefer a secure relationship with a person of their own sex, and the counsellor may help to find this.

Depression and loneliness are often closely connected, for

when a person is without much human contact he tends to concentrate upon himself and to become unduly upset by the ups and downs of life. The person who is depressed sees life in an entirely different light from other people and the extent to which his depression can be relieved by befriending depends very much on the type of depression. Everyone is depressed at one time or another, by such things as bereavement, failing an examination or by some trivial happening which seems to have great importance at the time. A friend can often help by showing that the catastrophe is not quite so bad as it seems, or by just listening and giving the impression that he too shares in the occurrence. But there are forms of depression which are far deeper than this, and then though a friend may help, he can do little to bring permanent relief.

Such forms of depression are usually found in conjunction with a particular personality structure. There may be a predisposition to reacting unfavourably to difficulties or problems. This type of person is usually the anxious type whose anxiety fluctuates widely. In pleasant surroundings or doing something which he normally enjoys it lifts for a time, but when difficulties or losses occur he is unduly upset and may be in the depths of depression. Another type of person is the one who has predisposing constitutional factors towards depression which are sometimes thought to be hereditary and which show themselves in a biochemical disturbance. Such a person usually suffers a very deep depression which may be totally incapacitating.

A counsellor should be able to distinguish the different types of depression fairly readily in order to refer those which he is unable to help to a psychiatrist. But the depression which has some obvious cause is well within his range of activity. He can help such a person by trying to get him to accept his depression for the time being on the grounds that it is a normal manifestation of the circumstances which have arisen, and will gradually pass. As the cause of the depression grows dimmer it should be possible to discover something which will take possession of the person and give a meaning to his life.

An important aspect of a depression is its degree, for the risk of suicide is usually associated with an intense depression. A useful guide to the severity of the depression is the capacity of the person to carry on his normal work or activity. If the depression prevents him from working this means that it is moderately severe or could be very severe, and this usually indicates the need for some medical advice.

The suicidal content of depression will vary from an unspecified lack of desire to go on living to ideas of suicide, fear of an impulse to kill oneself, and in severe depressive cases specifically working out how suicide can be achieved. It is usually quite possible to discuss suicide with a person without putting the idea into his mind or moving him a step nearer to putting it into practice. In fact it often helps a person to put into words the suicidal ideas that have been in the back of his mind. The counsellor can start by asking the person whether he has ever thought life not worth living, and then proceed gradually to discover whether he has actually thought of suicide, and if so a method.

Though there are communities where suicide is part of the cultural pattern, in the West it is regarded as socially and spiritually undesirable. Yet the numbers of suicides and attempted suicides are remarkably high. It is difficult to obtain any exact figures, for not all suicides are reported as such, and many who attempt suicide unsuccessfully are not known to have done so. But very generally in Britain at the present time about 5,000 men and women do succeed in killing themselves each year, and another 30,000 to 40,000 try to do so. Many of these are depressives, the elderly, the isolated and the alcoholic.

The counsellor will come into contact with some potential suicides, but there are many others who would not visit him. It is here again that befriending organisations can be of great help, in their closer contact with such people and in sorting out those who do need medical and counselling help from the temporarily depressed. The most well known of these organisations is the Samaritans which was started in 1953 at St Stephen's, Walbrook, in the City of London, and has now spread to many other cities both in this country and abroad. The Samaritans offer, in the first instance, a telephone line to those tempted to suicide and despair, and then a friend who will share or alleviate their burden. In London alone, more than 3,000 people a year call the Samaritan telephone number. They need not give their name, but the Samaritan helper to whom they talk will try to win their confidence and persuade them to come and discuss their troubles. An urgent night call will usually result in a Samaritan going to the person, while the outcome of a day call may be a visit to the nearest Samaritan office. If counselling is necessary an appointment will be made with one of the Samaritan consultants, and if a visit to a doctor is required this will be arranged. But quite often it is a case for befriending and then one of the Samaritans will be allocated for this purpose, and will keep in touch with the person until he is able to cope with his problems again.

Samaritans are not necessarily church members, or even Christians, though some groups of Samaritans are connected with a particular church. It is the power to befriend another person which is the first qualification for a Samaritan and not his form of belief. A few churches have formed their own groups of 'samaritans' whose purpose usually is to befriend in the first place, and to follow this up with material, psychological, medical and spiritual help. Such groups tend to be confined to a parish or local area, and they follow methods suited to the neighbourhood which they serve.

Loneliness and depression are often the result of agoraphobia which is an intense and obsessive anxiety at leaving the shelter of a house and of meeting other people. The condition tends to be common among married women between the ages of thirty and fifty and they are often gifted people of above average intelligence but apt to be anxious and sensitive with a great deal of imagination and too much time on their hands. The Christian Telephone Ministry, which uses the same medium as the Samaritans, befriends such people by putting them in touch with a telephone friend who will ring up periodically until a friendship is established. It is then hoped that there will be an invitation to call, to visit periodically and eventually to go out together.

Befriending on a mutual basis is the purpose of an association known as 'The Open Door'. Members try to help one another in a number of practical ways, such as transport for treatment or essential journeys, or by friendly and supportive telephone calls in time of stress. Sometimes they pool experiences of successful ways of helping to allay their fears. This type of help cannot, of course, cure severe cases of agoraphobia which is generally an indication of a deep underlying and persistent state of anxiety. But it can be of great use to those who are only mildly afflicted and who would like to end their enforced solitude but dare not take the step alone. It is often combined with medical treatment, and some hospitals make use of befriending services of this type.

ALCOHOLICS AND DRUG ADDICTS

The weary, anxious and lonely may look for help not from other people, but from some form of narcotic which will dull their senses and give them for a time a feeling of well-being. Alcohol has been used for this purpose for a very long time and drugs are now becoming fashionable in this country, partly because improved communications have made them more readily available and the law as yet has not stood very strongly in their way, and partly because they offer a novel and often more exciting way of forgetting troubles and problems.

Harmful drinking is very much a matter of degree. Most people drink moderately, and some from time to time get drunk, usually at parties or important celebrations. These are said to be social drinkers. But some people drink excessively, and this is shown either by the frequency with which they become intoxicated, or by the social, economic or medical consequences of their continual intake of alcohol. Not all excessive drinkers are alcoholics though probably the great majority of them proceed to this next stage. Alcoholics are those who are unable spontaneously to give up drinking. Though they may go without a drink for a few days, or sometimes for even longer periods, inevitably they revert. The greater the need to stop drinking the more difficult they find it to do so. Most alcoholics proceed to a further stage where their brains or their bodies have been so harmed by alcohol that the effects persist even when they are not drinking, and then they are regarded as chronic alcoholics.

It is difficult to estimate the magnitude of the problem of alcoholism, for it is neither a notifiable disease nor is it definable in unambiguous terms. Many alcoholics do not come to any organisation interested in helping them, and medical practitioners are not always aware of them among their patients. The World Health Organisation in 1952 estimated that there were some 350,000 alcoholics in Britain and the convictions for drinking have shown a steep increase in recent years, especially for young people. Alcoholism is, therefore, a fairly serious problem and poses many social difficulties both for the community and for the alcoholic himself and his family. In most cities there are depressed areas where chronic alcoholics congregate and eke out a poverty-stricken, degenerate and sometimes psychotic existence. Less severe alcoholism leads to absenteeism, and unemployment, debt, crime, social decline and child neglect. While the average family spends about four per cent of its weekly income on drink, in an alcoholic's household as much as ten times this amount may be used for this purpose.

Many and varied influences combine to generate alcoholism, and there is usually no single cause. Physical causes, such as endocrine and nutritional factors have been suggested, but without much proof. Social and cultural theories are perhaps stronger. Higher wages and greater leisure can lead to more drinking. So can the customs of the community and the example of friends and neighbours. But perhaps most important of all is the personality of the alcoholic. Certain people appear predisposed to alcoholism by some prior impairment in their personality structure. Such people exploit the gratification and the relief from tension which drinking confers, because these psychic accompaniments of addictive drinking make their problems in living more tolerable. They are usually people who are unable to get sufficient reward from ordinary living.

Counselling does not help all types of alcoholics, and therefore it is important for the counsellor to determine to what degree his skills are adequate for each specific situation. Counselling can often be of help at an early stage, before a person has become an alcohol addict. Though it is quite obvious to others that a person is an excessive drinker, he himself is often not aware of the fact. A counsellor can help such a person to recognise that alcohol lies at the root of many of his personal and social difficulties, and he may be able to suggest appropriate treatment and medical care before drinking has gained a firm grip upon a person. A minister, doctor, or social worker is often in contact with such people and though it is by no means easy to suggest to a person that he is drinking excessively, it can save him from serious trouble later on.

No clear distinction of alcoholics into types is possible, but very general groups can be indicated, with their respective responses to counselling. A group which is unlikely to respond to counselling at all, or who will only benefit when drinking has been interrupted, are the neurotic alcoholics who drink to diminish their emotional conflicts. Their principal disorder is in fact neurosis, and alcoholism is merely the most evident disturbance. Their drinking represents an attempt to cure symptoms of the underlying condition. Treatment, therefore, has to deal first with the psychological disorder, and then perhaps a counsellor can help with readjustment into society.

Symptomatic alcoholism is somewhat similar, since in this case the person is also suffering from another complaint of which drinking is only an indication. Alcoholism can be a symptom which brings to notice people suffering from depression or schizophrenia, and from psychiatric illness due to brain disease. Then all that can be done is to treat this underlying psychiatric condition. Quite a number of such people are mentally subnormal. They may never have achieved a success in a job, perhaps not married, may be in and out of prison and frequent the fringe areas of big cities where heavy drinking is the pattern of the sub-society to which they belong. They cause continual trouble to clergy, social workers and to all who try to help them, and there seems to be no one way of doing so. Individual befriending may be an answer for a time, but is rarely permanently successful.

On the other hand there is quite a large group who can respond to counselling. They are those who have demonstrated competence in their careers, in family and community relationships and in other areas which normally require some degree of social adjustment. They are at least of average intelligence, are sensitive to their responsibilities and have some capacity for developing and maintaining interpersonal relations. Yet they are constantly under stress. Their accomplishments may have been achieved with considerable effort and they may live in fear of not making the grade. Or they may set their standards too high and be unable achieve what they would like. A variety of circumstances may lead to their distress which they assuage by small amounts of alcohol. They appear to be psychologically vulnerable to the effects of alcohol, and so what starts as a social situation develops into repetitive and excessive drinking until they are unable to abstain from it. Sometimes it takes the form of regular heavy yet restrained drinking. People like this often sit by themselves hour after hour in the public house to escape the family's antagonism. Others are solitary drinkers at home, and if they are women they will generally do so in secret. They may engage in drinking bouts which can continue for hours, days or weeks, ending only with physical or financial exhaustion or when interrupted at home or in hospital. Such people are often compulsive drinkers. Once they have started they cannot stop and they go on until all their money is spent or their supplies are finished, or until an accident or unconsciousness intervenes. This type of alcoholic usually gets himself into serious social difficulties. His drunken behaviour repels. He alienates and antagonises those who come into contact with him, including his relatives, friends and workmates, and this will be so even when they are trying to help him.

The aim in the treatment of alcoholism is to achieve a realignment of the emotional forces within the personality, so that the need to use alcohol because of internal and external pressures is reduced. This is a long-term process but it is an attainable goal for many of the alcoholics in the last mentioned group, and the counsellor can usually be of great help.

At the first interview the counsellor has to discover the drinking pattern – that is whether the person is a daily drinker, an episodic drinker or an intermittent drinker or one given to bouts. This pattern will provide clues to emotional stresses which underlie the drinking. An important function of this interview is to determine the nature of the situation which brought him to the counsellor and the circumstances in which recent drinking has taken place, for it is unlikely for him to be able to improve while the immediate situation holds threats for him. He needs to be helped to work out a plan of action to cope with the environmental pressures which surround him. On the other hand, the counsellor should be ready at this first interview to refer him to a doctor or a hospital if the situation appears to be one which he is not competent to handle. More harm than good would be done if he tried to counsel a seriously disturbed psychoneurotic, or a latent schizophrenic.

Some alcoholics in the early stages of recovery set themselves goals which they find impossible to achieve. Effective counselling should keep them from doing this. It can also help them when a drinking episode occurs after a period of abstention. Many alcoholics experience mood swings during which the desire for a drink becomes overruling. The counsellor can judge the length of such swings, help the alcoholic to understand their nature and fix another interview around the time when one is likely to occur.

Many alcoholics achieve a level of stability without ever understanding the forces which impelled them to drink, but others have an unusual knowledge of their emotional difficulties. Interpretation by the counsellor of the person's motivation, feelings and reactions should be given sparingly, and only when he is psychologically able to benefit from them. The way to recovery is experiencing rather than knowing, and as the alcoholic is able to reduce the length and increase the timing of his bouts so he will be encouraged to go ahead and be able to assume more and more independence. There is usually no complete recovery until he has learnt that he must not have even one drink. Therefore he is never really 'cured' but is enabled to live in society without the prop of alcohol. This is what the total abstinence movement of the nineteenth century made clear, and it is here that spiritual help can be of the greatest use.

Many alcoholics find great assistance in group therapy. Alcoholics Anonymous, which they run themselves, provides this on a mutual basis, and it is said that at least half their number find relief at the first meeting and somewhat less than a quarter are failures. To use their own description, they are 'a fellowship of men and women who share their experience, strength and hope with each other that they may solve their common problem and help others to recover from alcoholism'. The movement was started in America by members of the Oxford Group and they use as a basis for their work the familiar principles of open self-scrutiny, admission of defects, aid to others and making reparation for harm done in the past. It is not a religious institution but its group therapy and its twelve steps to recovery have a definite religious basis. It recognises that will-power alone cannot conquer the craving for alcohol, its members admit their powerlessness to do so, they realise that alcoholism is a disease and they admit that it has no cure but that it can be arrested. There is no question of controlled drinking. Their object in the first place is to keep entirely sober for the current twenty-four hours and then to extend this period as they are able. In order to achieve this they admit that there is a power greater than themselves, which most of them call God, which can control their behaviour when they themselves are powerless.

There are groups in most cities and, to join, it is merely necessary to want to stop drinking and be prepared to admit that one is powerless to do so. At the meetings members describe their successes and failures since the last meeting, discuss difficulties common to all, and one or more members will usually relate the story of former drinking days and successful recovery. Each newcomer is assigned a sponsor who is an A.A. member who has stopped drinking and his function is to come to the aid of the new member whenever necessary and to stay with him for as long as he is needed. Thus the alcoholic who succeeds with the help of A.A. has a constant body of people who share his interest in staying sober and many A.A. members find that the movement becomes their overriding life concern.

Alcoholics Anonymous achieves least success with those who are not gregarious and cannot tolerate the pressures towards continuous and intimate relationships with others. Others do not like the relish with which some recount their drinking history, and some dislike the religious emphasis. But the success of the movement has led many doctors and psychiatrists to suggest that their patients should join. There are groups of A.A. at some of the mental hospitals which have alcoholic units and in some cases alcoholics combine A.A. membership with psychiatric and drug treatment.

The counsellor cannot overlook the needs of the wife and family of the alcoholic, for they have frequently suffered greatly and need help perhaps as much as the alcoholic himself. Living in association with an alcoholic is a traumatic experience. From the wife's standpoint her husband will not be dependable. She will have to manage the greater part of the household responsibilities on her own. She cannot rely on him to play his part either in making important decisions about such things as the children's education or simply day-to-day choices such as planning leisure activities. Usually she will have to go out to work, and when her husband is unemployed she is the breadwinner. Socially too he is no longer dependable and she never knows when he will be home for meals. She cannot arrange to go out to friends, nor dare she invite them to the house. She has to witness his intoxicated behaviour, to endure his violence and accept his jealousies.

It is not usually wise for the counsellor to talk about the wife and family at the early interviews for it is the person himself who feels he needs help and so should be encouraged to take some immediate action of his own. He needs to feel that he is doing something about his problems independently of his wife and friends. It is only when he consents that they should be considered and perhaps a joint interview arranged. The wife herself may need counselling in order to help her to understand her own feelings when her husband begins to recover. The competent wife who has been used to making all the decisions and to handling the finances of the family is not always ready to surrender these responsibilities when her husband is ready and eager to resume them. She will usually say that she fears that if he relapses once again, he will plunge them into the chaos from which they were slowly and painfully rescued by her exertions, and this of course may happen. She may not realise that often she has come to enjoy the authority in the family which the situation has imposed on her. Things like this need to be talked through with the counsellor and ways of gradually returning to the equilibrium which existed before he became an alcoholic need to be explored. New friends will often have to be made, new employment found, and even a change of school for the children. All these things can be discussed with the counsellor and they are usually best talked over with him by husband and wife together.

Drug addiction bears many resemblances to alcoholism, although the number of drug addicts is far less. The publicity with regard to drug taking is partly due to the fact that it is predominant among young people, and partly because of its dire consequences. Alcohol itself is a drug, although like tea, coffee and tobacco it is a socially acceptable one. The older drugs, such as opium and hemp and the newer synthetic ones are those which are regarded as socially undesirable. Drugs can be conveniently divided into the hard or dangerous restricted drugs, and those which are soft. The former include heroin and cocaine; the latter the barbiturates or 'sleepers', the amphetamines or 'thrusters' which keep the user awake, elevate the mood and induce a feeling of well-being, and cannabis and LSD which tend to cause hallucinations.

Addiction to the soft drugs may produce effects fairly similar to those of alcoholism. It is with the hard drugs that the differences are found. The person who takes these drugs needs to go on increasing their intake in order to get the desired effect. When he stops physiological changes set up a subjective need for more of the drug, and so he experiences a craving. He also develops withdrawal symptoms which are promptly alleviated by another single dose. But this gives only temporary relief, and the dose has to be repeated at regular intervals if the symptoms are not to reappear. It is the intensity of these symptoms and the need for increasing quantities of the drug which distinguish the hard from the soft drugs and from alcohol.

There are various reasons which lead to the start of drug taking. Sometimes a person depends on a drug in order to conform to the behaviour and standards of his particular community. There is always a small proportion of people who find life more difficult to live than the majority. Such a person has often had an insecure childhood and has difficulty in learning how to adjust to the demands of life. He longs to be able to enjoy himself at social functions as other people do, but he is too inhibited and self-conscious. He finds that the depressant effect of sedatives releases him from his inhibitions, or pep pills boost his self-confidence. Either way he is enabled to cope, but afterwards he suffers a marked reaction.

In other cases a person depends upon a drug to provide enjoyment or to suppress or come to terms with his mental or emotional conflicts. People who have never learnt to develop satisfying emotional relationships or who have never discovered how to enjoy themselves will demand intense stimuli to experience any satisfaction at all. The same is true of those who want to experience more pleasure from the finer cultural achievements and creations of man or nature. Hence loudness, violence or intensity of emotion are demanded and accepted as common place. Drugs provide the subjective sensations which they demand and normal life is found to be quite unacceptable after such stimulation. The result is that drugs are increasingly taken to prevent their intense and protracted periods of boredom. It is not surprising that people of an older generation, brought up to the gentler enjoyments, find this mentality difficult to understand.

Those who have mental or emotional conflicts may suffer worries and anxieties in secret rather than face their personal problems and work through them with the advice and help of friends. They are perhaps too proud or too ashamed to admit that they need help. Their problems may involve faulty human relationships and to discuss them with the sort of adults or parents who have old-fashioned or preconceived ideas is impossible. Thus a person may hide his anxieties under a blanket of barbiturates or cannabis, or he may distort them out of all recognition by LSD. Having hidden his problems he needs the drug continually to keep them hidden. Hence he becomes dependent upon the drug and less inclined to face his problems.

When the body becomes dependent upon the presence of the drug for its normal functioning, then the person has become a drug addict or a compulsive drug taker. Opium and its derivatives, morphine and heroin, are most likely to cause this state, for when absorbed into the body they compete with the naturally occurring substances and gradually replace them in the normal chemical processes of life, in the body's cells. The result of this is tolerance which demands a steadily increasing dose to produce the same effect, withdrawal symptoms in the form of physical pain, extreme anxiety, apprehension and perhaps delusions of persecution if the dose is stopped, reduced or even delayed, and an intense craving for the drug so that the addict becomes entirely absorbed with the task of ensuring that the next dose will be available in a few hours when the dreaded symptoms begin to develop again. Even though these physical symptoms may be very severe, the real problem for the addict is the continual yearning for the drug and this is really an aspect of the psychic dependence which the drug produces.

Drug dependence is essentially a relationship between a personality and a drug and this accounts for the wide variations in effect and experience that occur. The physically and mentally healthy person does not need drugs, and the vast majority of young people are of this type and are able to develop a responsible attitude to life provided the adult world is reasonably tolerant and understanding. Three factors seem to combine to make people dependent on drugs. There must be a basic personality weakness, either inherited or acquired in some way. This personality must experience a crisis of some sort; and at that moment the drug must be available. Most unstable young people in a healthy social atmosphere will steer their way through their difficulties and ultimately become reasonably stable adults. But if drugs are fashionable and easily available then they may be encouraged to try them and so come to depend upon them as artificial props at a time when they should be developing their own independence and self-reliance.

The first encounter with pep pills containing amphetamine is usually at coffee bars, clubs, parties or dances where the person may also be introduced to cannabis. Toleration will develop quickly and the initial one or two pills in an evening will become ten or twenty. Though the young person may know that such pills are illegal, since the practice is common among his friends his respect for the law and the police is weakened. His basic personality problems remain the same, and while under the influence of these pills he may fall an easy prey to the pedlars or 'pushers' of heroin. At first sniffs or injections are given free, but after a time the 'pusher' demands payment. If the drug taker cannot offer it and has to decline further doses he is, in a few hours, in the misery of withdrawal symptoms and becomes prepared to buy another dose at any cost. Thus the person has become a drug addict, and from now on his life is preoccupied with finding the next dose. For a while he may keep his addiction secret, thinking he can break free without help, but he soon discovers that he cannot. He is now 'hooked' and utterly dependent upon his supplier.

To help those under the influence of drugs, the first step has to be to win the person's confidence so that he begins to want to be free of his dependence upon them. Unless he will co-operate cure is impossible, and in the case of some addicts they do not want to be cured because life without the support of a drug is worse than the problems which drug taking involves.

Such people need psychiatric help with their fundamental problems before they will attempt to seek a cure. This is usually the case with those on heroin.

People dependent upon the soft drugs can usually have the drug withdrawn without much difficulty providing their underlying problems can be solved. Here there is great scope for the counsellor for in most cases the dependence can be overcome with the support and advice of a well-informed person with whom the drug taker is willing to share his or her problems. But if intense psychic dependence has developed, the matter is much more difficult and will need the help of a trained psychiatrist.

The problem posed by the hard drugs, particularly heroin, is far more difficult on account of the prolonged compulsive craving and the physical dependence which this produces. Treatment usually takes place in hospital, and may last as long as a year or more. Observation is first made to assess his personal problems and his genuine drug needs. Then some form of withdrawal is followed, and supplemented by rehabilitation, at first in the hospital and then in a residential hostel where the person slowly readjusts to life without his drug and begins to sort out his personality problems. He has to learn how to live with people again, and perhaps be taught a new job. His greatest difficulty may be to accept the society which he had previously rejected.

Psychotherapy will play a critical part in this, but there is also the need throughout the whole of the treatment process for the support of an understanding person who will perhaps befriend him until he reaches the point where he wants to be rid of his heroin, and then continue to visit him throughout his treatment, to help him during his period of rehabilitation, and to remain in touch with him for a long time afterwards. For the intense craving will never entirely leave him, and will return in times of stress or be aggravated by memories, familiar places, acquaintances, publicity and even by being asked about his drug taking. Something must fill the void left by the heroin, and so new friends, occupations and activities are essential. The pastoral counsellor, provided he is knowledgeable about the facts of drug addiction and their effects, has an important part to play here. Not only can he offer his counselling services at the appropriate time, which will often mean working closely with the psychotherapist, but with the support of helpers, he can provide a caring atmosphere, can meet the social needs of the person and can be on call in an emergency.

Perhaps the greatest need of all is to help a person before he reaches the stage of drug taking. Each individual has to discover that he is a person who matters, who can find fulfilment in life and can relate to others with confidence. But this discovery may take many years and is not always made easily, especially by those who for one reason or another are less privileged. It is, therefore, important that a counsellor or person in charge of any organisation or group should be aware of those who are at risk and be ready to help them to face their difficulties, to accept them and to overcome them. Those who feel inadequate have to discover that there is a field in which they can make a contribution and be valued, and those who are bored and disillusioned must be helped to realise that there are opportunities to live full and adventurous lives. This is where the clergyman, teacher or social worker becomes involved, for he is likely to meet people at this stage. Instead of adopting the somewhat critical and condemning attitude which is commonly found, he can provide an understanding and an opportunity to talk which may be the one thing needed to help the person at this particular moment, and so together they may be able to work out other ways of meeting the difficulties and problems with which the person is faced.

IX. Counselling in Groups

The usual method of counselling is that of the dialogue, but sometimes it is more suitable to use the group. This may happen when the counsellor's time is restricted and he has several people whom he feels could be helped together. It is a method which was frequently used during the last war for those who had been affected by its pressures. Another use for group counselling is to meet the needs of people who seek help with problems involving their relationships with several people. It may then be advantageous to get the people together and to 'thrash out the problem' as it were, with the counsellor present. Occasionally the group is a more suitable way of dealing with certain age groups, when it is necessary to convey information which could be embarrassing in a dialogue. This is often so with adolescents who feel greater security in a group than they would in a personal conversation.

Group methods will vary with the people and types of problem involved, but in general the group method differs from that of individual counselling in that the counsellor cannot give his undivided attention to one person. He is concerned as well with the functioning of the group, for this is the main helping agency. But this does not mean that he ignores the person in favour of the group. The individual member is still the object of help, but this help comes through interaction with the group rather than in dialogue with the counsellor. Nevertheless, group counselling still relies on verbal communications, but these will be not only with the group counsellor, but also between members of the group itself. The counsellor's job, as leader of the group, will be to guide the conversation of the group along lines that will be of use to the different members. He may need to know the members personally, although this is not always necessary when the purpose of the group is problem-centred rather than person-centred.

This distinction between problem-centred and person-centred serves to distinguish between two different types of groups, the supportive group and the helping group. The purpose of a group that is supportive is to enable its members to deal with some common problem more adequately. A helping group will try to give its members a new outlook which should enable each one to become more able to deal with his own particular situation. This distinction, however, is by no means clear-cut, for many a supportive group will also be helping, and a helping group is frequently supportive as well.

The helping group will usually be fairly small, perhaps five or six people, and it will meet reasonably regularly although rarely more frequently than once a week. Its processes will resemble that of individual counselling in that its first need will be to gain insight, and then to find a way of using this insight to determine behaviour. The members who come will be troubled about some similar problem. They may have conflicts about it which need to be bared and irrational ways of behaviour which they can discuss together. In these ways some sort of insight may be gained into their difficulties. Quite often an idea arises which is foreign to the thinking of most of the members, and this will need to be assimilated. The effect should be to bring about some sort of change in the feelings of members about their problem to themselves, or to the others, or to the group as a whole.

The first meeting of the group, like that of counselling, depends very much upon the atmosphere conveyed. The leader has to take an active part at this stage in introducing its members and in helping them to understand a little about the ways in which groups work. The members will often wait respectfully for some instruction or direction from the leader, may ask him

o

directly for some guidance about procedure and may be very surprised when they find that this is not laid down but that they have come to discuss their own problem with one another and so it is up to them to talk about it in their own way.

Verbalising a problem is often more difficult in a group than it is to a counsellor in private, for not only do words have to be found for feelings, but there is always the attitude of the group to take into account, and less personal encouragement is possible from the leader. But once the first difficulty of talking to the group is over, the fact that others are doing the same thing acts as an incentive. Fairly soon the members will get down to discussing their individual difficulties and they will find that they have so many in common that any sense of isolation or peculiarity will wear off. As one member talks about the feeling of a problem to himself the others will consider whether they feel the same and the extent to which their feelings differ. In this way they come to understand themselves more deeply and thoroughly and perhaps to discover some new meaning to their attitudes and conflicts.

The next stage is when the group has more truly become an entity. They no longer look to the leader in any moment of indecision or insecurity, although they remain conscious of his presence. Instead of just talking about their own experiences they address one another and respond to one another. They begin to question each other's feelings, and to try to discover why they are so and whether some slightly different approach might not be better. One or two of the members may talk more confidentially together and for a time form a small sub-group. This will be because they feel they have something in common and can make some use of it together. They are beginning to gain an insight into their problem.

The final stage, like that of counselling, is how to apply this insight that they have gained to themselves, and this will vary with each different member. They will now discuss it against their own backgrounds, against their past successes and failures, and in the light of what they have learnt. They may argue and they may despair, but they should make some progress, and they will at least have some new ideas. The leader may have to be a little more active at this stage, for the members need to form realistic plans for the future, and ones which will stand alone when the prop of the group meetings is removed. This may present fewer difficulties than in individual counselling, for group meetings are less abstract and so less divorced from ordinary life.

When the group is supportive, as for example a group of people who have recently lost their husbands and come to talk over their common problems, a fairly comfortable size is about a dozen to fifteen people. This will preserve a certain amount of anonymity without losing the feeling of belongingness. Such a group is small enough for the member to be accepted personally, to be able to talk, to be listened to sympathetically and to share with others and yet not so small that the person feels that his privacy is invaded and that he is being required to say more than he wants.

The supportive group will follow a similar pattern to the helping group, but with less delving into motives and inner compulsions. The first two stages will be shorter, especially the second, and the third far longer for in this the members will discuss in greater detail how they have dealt with their difficulties so far and how suitable these methods may be for some other member who is interested in them. The leader in this sort of group may have far less to do, for the members, once they have got to know one another, will tend to take the lead themselves and to be able to reject what is unsuitable and to retain the more relevant suggestions.

A supportive group for young people is usually more informative in nature. It almost verges on a teaching group, although it does so without applying its information. Facts are offered in a way which is suitable for the particular age group and the various ways of response of the members are discussed. The members are then encouraged to decide for themselves what attitudes they think they should follow, but they are not usually left in doubt as to the approach of the leader.

Quite often, with young people, it is possible to combine individual with group counselling. Key topics are then discussed in the group and the relevant information made available. Such topics will be about matters such as the use of alcohol, drugs or smoking, intercourse before marriage, or sexual attitudes in general. These discussions will tend to be more instructive than is usual in group counselling, and to refer to the normal customs of society and the general attitudes to morality and sexual standards. In the individual counselling the young person will be helped to use what he has learnt to solve his own particular problem, not so much in order to help him to fit into society as to equip him to make decisions which are most suitable to his stage of development. It is during these individual sessions that problems of anxiety and of conflict are likely to arise and the counsellor will deal with them in the usual manner of personal counselling.

With adults it is not so usual to combine individual with group counselling for adults are expected to be able to bring their anxieties and conflicts to the group and to find an insight into them there. It is when the complexes seem too serious or are likely to be disturbing to the group that the counsellor will see particular members on their own. The advantage of the individual session is that it is possible to get back to infancy or a far earlier period of time, while the group session is concerned almost entirely with the present or near past or future. The difficulties for the member lie in the return to the group. For he may have got out of touch with the group, and will certainly find it disconcerting to be at one moment looking at matters from a vertical or depth approach and at another on a horizontal level. Only the skill of the leader will help with this and will prevent it from delaying the progress of the group. Experience has shown that if individual counselling is required it should either precede or follow group counselling rather than that there should be a concurrent use of both. The general exception is when all the members of a group are also receiving individual counselling at the same time.

Much of the success of a group depends upon the group counsellor. Though he is a member of the group he participates in the life of the group in a more complex way than the other members. He has to watch his own reactions both to the individual members and to the group as a whole. He will keep to himself his insight into his own feelings, but his insight into the individual reactions he will use to increase his understanding of the group as a whole. He will help the group to interpret the insight that they gain and he will encourage individual members to do the same, and in this he will use tactics very similar to those of the individual counsellor, the use of pertinent remarks and of the throwing back of questions upon the person himself. In this way the group should become more sensitive and sophisticated about the way it is working and individual members should become more knowledgeable about their reactions within the group and also within themselves.

The type and degree of leadership will vary with the counsellor's own personality and the needs of the group. He must be able to develop their interest in active and enthusiastic participation in the group's affairs, and to create a spirit of mutual tolerance so that the members will feel able to say what they think without reservations. At first everything will depend upon his leadership, but if it is successful then the group should develop forces within itself which will be capable of taking over, and so free the leader to pay more attention to the needs of individual members. Some leaders will set out to manage a group more than others, because they believe that matters cannot be left entirely to the group and that the leader must be constantly in touch with the group and vigilant in its direction. Other leaders will be ready to allow the group to determine its own affairs and may interfere only when some severe disagreement or difficulty occurs.

A group does not necessarily need a leader and there are groups, known as mutual groups, which are completely leaderless in their make-up. They are usually of a supportive rather than a helping nature and are concerned with some particular problem which is common to the group and realised as such by them all. This problem is not usually one in which an unknown solution has to be found, but one of readjustment where the need is to help the members of the group to fit more easily into the circumstances in which they find themselves.

One of the earliest and probably the most well known of the mutual groups is Alcoholics Anonymous. Their purpose, as was suggested in the previous chapter, is to bring together those who are unable to stop excessive drinking and through group support to help them to remain sober. The meetings, which are held regularly, are intended to give a feeling of coherence and solidarity to the members and each brings his own experiences and the ways he has tried to solve them to the meetings in the hope that others will help him and that he in his turn may be able to help others.

These mutual groups are becoming a very usual method of dealing with types of problems which are commonly found throughout the community. Parents of unmarried mothers, those with children at approved schools, deserted wives, and similar groups find support and help in this way. Instead of having to work through their practical problems on their own they can get guidance from the ways in which others have dealt with such problems. The same is true of many conscious emotional difficuclties. It is when things tend to become complicated and go below the level of consciousness that such a mutual group is of little help. It is then that a counsellor is needed who is able to exercise some control over the deeper emotions and to help to direct them in the way of useful purposes. It is quite usual for members of a mutual group who are finding things particularly difficult to seek the help of a counsellor to tide them over the difficulty but still to attend the meetings of the group and to find benefit from doing so. The difference between this and a similar situation with a helping group is that a mutual group is much more concerned with practical matters, while the helping group is itself dealing with submerged problems.

Some groups can be described as occupational in that they are organised around some particular activity. They may be engaged in a physical activity such as tennis, rambling or dancing, in creative activity such as art, music or play reading, or they may be educational in the sense of focusing on talks, discussions or films. But whatever the occupation, the sense of belonging and participating in the group activities can have a therapeutic significance which gives each person in the group an opportunity to develop and utilise his faculties and skills with a purpose in view and so enables him to feel secure and overcome any tendencies to egocentricity.

The counsellor, if he is the pastor of a church, is usually concerned with organisational groups that have been consciously formed to serve some particular purpose and which are carefully structured to achieve this. Church organisational groups will often have a hierarchy of authority, certain disciplines and restraints which are rigorously applied and some control over the membership of the group and what use is made of it.

The chief organisational group which the pastor has is his congregation. Though he is the leader of this, he is not entirely free to control it as he likes, for a congregation is usually part of a wider organisation or denomination which lays down certain rules and precepts that the individual congregation is expected to follow. Within the congregation, however, the pastor has a freer hand with regard to the groups that are formed. The youth club, the young wives, the club for the elderly and other similar clubs can usually be organised with a reasonable degree of flexibility to meet the needs of their members, and these needs will vary with the people whom they serve. But they tend to be need-centred rather than person-centred, and those who fall within the ambit of the organisations but do not have that particular need are unlikely to join or, if they do, are unlikely to remain very long as members. There will also be occasional and temporary groups which the pastor will form for some specified purpose, as for example a group of those to be married in the church at some future specified date.

These groups can and should be used both for the members of the congregation and for those outside. For the members of the congregation such groups are largely supportive, that is they enable their members to carry out more easily and satisfactorily both the aims of the church and the living of their own lives. It is assumed that if any member requires more specific care than the group can provide the counselling services of the pastor are available. In this way there is built up a group of people who are secure within themselves and so able to receive others who may be in need of such security and friendship.

Thus the groups that are supportive to the members of a church can be therapeutic to the outsider. They should be able to offer warmth and comfort alike to those who need these things for their health and for their well-being. Because the members are secure in themselves they should be able to accept those who are less secure and to help them to reach the state which they themselves have attained, largely through the group contacts which the church has offered them. This is how it is possible for the pastor who is also a counsellor to have an extra source of help in the form of an accepting community to which he can recommend those who come to him for help.

This is of great importance today when the tendency is to

shift the emphasis of the care for those who are unwell on to the community rather than the hospital. Both the physically and the mentally ill spend a comparatively short time away from home, and return long before they are able to settle down to their ordinary work and way of living. It is here that the group organisation can be of great help to them, as a halfway house between hospital and home, as an accepting community where they will be able to find help with their difficulties of adjustment and as a support when they find this adjustment exceedingly troublesome. The church group is particularly suited for this purpose.

Thus the pastoral counsellor is enabled to use both the dialogue and the group methods of counselling, and although his main resource will be the dialogue he will be enabled to supplement it with the group. If he is the pastor of a church he will have at hand groups which should be suitable for the reception of those he counsels himself and for the many other people who find themselves in need of some therapeutic group or community which will support them over a period of difficulty.

X. The Pastoral Approach

An understanding of personal relationships is the basis of counselling, whatever form the counselling may take. The counsellor and the person he is helping have to reach the intimacy of a dialogue, and in this intimacy work out together how best the person shall proceed. In pastoral counselling the relationship which the counsellor has to foster is not only that between the person and himself, but also that between the person and God. Pastoral counselling regards the human being in the dimensions of body, mind and spirit, and only when these three are working in conjunction and functioning aright can wholeness or maturity arise within the person. The pastoral counsellor has to try to help the person who comes to him to develop this integration in his personality.

It is sometimes thought that there are carefully designed techniques to bring this about, and that all that the would-be counsellor has to do is to master these techniques. Thus ways are suggested as to how to conduct an interview, how to deal with the person who says very little, what methods should be used with the alcoholic, and so on. In fact it is thought possible to have a detailed guide book which tells the counsellor how to respond on every conceivable occasion.

For adequate counselling this is not the case. There are no hard and fast rules or methods which should be followed, and it is never possible to decide beforehand exactly what plan of action should take place. There are, however, certain basic principles of approach which make it easier for a counsellor to form a relationship within which he can help a person. Many of those engaged in counselling as part of their work feel very diffident as to their ability to get closer to a person and are intensely aware of the fact that they do not know what to say or do. This very soon communicates itself with the result that any sort of dialogue becomes overwhelmingly difficult. The counselling methods which are suggested are intended to help the counsellor to rise above these difficulties and to enable him more easily to get into contact with a person and win his confidence.

Once this contact is formed the counsellor has to look both to the particular needs which the person presents and to the personality of the person himself, for needs have to be met and the way in which this is best achieved depends essentially upon the reactions of the person who has come for counselling. Needs often show themselves in conflict and anxiety, although this is not always the case, and the counsellor has to be able to discern between the straightforward needs of a person and those that are deeper. His knowledge of psychology and psychological methods may enable him to help with the latter form of need, provided the need is not too deep, but he has to beware not to jump to hasty conclusions. A little knowledge of psychology may make a counsellor think he knows at once why something has happened. The wise counsellor will take a long time before he makes such a decision, and even when he has his suspicions he will not convey these to the person he is counselling. Good counselling leads a person to discover such things for himself.

Counselling will never take the same form with any two people even though the need may be the same. For each person is unique in himself and will respond in his own way to approaches that are made. The counsellor will be helped by knowing something of the general types of people, but hindered if he starts by categorising them. Types may give the initial clues, but on these he has to build up the unique characteristics which each individual possesses. This is perhaps the hardest part of counselling and the counsellor needs to be very sensitive to any mistakes he may make, for once a person feels that he is not fully understood any further efforts at counselling are wasted. A good counsellor will spend unlimited effort in trying to find a common ground with those he is counselling, and if this fails he is well advised to suggest some other counsellor.

The techniques of counselling cannot be applied in isolation for they need to be combined with a very careful study of the background of the person involved and of the special situation in which he finds himself. Since everyone is a member of the community in which he lives and works and takes part in the activities of various groups in this community he will find himself playing a variety of roles. The counsellor needs to be aware of these things and be able to judge to what extent they are affecting the person's behaviour. He should know his community and its components as someone who has gone among the different people who comprise it and entered into their feelings and attitudes. If he is dealing with some particular group of people then this is possible, but the counsellor who has a wide variety of people coming to him will have to acquire some of this knowledge through reading, and there are a number of sociological surveys which will help him in this way.

The situation in which a person finds himself may be an indication of some interior conflict or difficulty, but it can also be due to some particular circumstances or to some patch of misfortune. Hence the importance of being quite clear as to exactly what the situation is. Some very serious situations can be resolved by a relaxation of surrounding circumstances, and even if there is a deeper cause a change in circumstances may alleviate the anxiety and enable the person to deal with his troubles more easily.

In this way counselling overlaps a number of different disciplines or skills. It makes some use of medical knowledge, especially that in the field of psychiatry. It is also closely related to social work for social caseworkers have been helping people through interpersonal relationships for many years. It is linked with

THE PASTORAL APPROACH

pastoral theology for 'the cure of souls' and until recently has been almost entirely in the hands of the Christian minister.

The doctor, the social worker and the clergy each have their contributions to make in this new process of counselling. The methods which the social worker follows and the needs which the pastor and the medical practitioner have in the furtherance of their work are complementary. Religion and medicine can also offer insights into some of the basic assumptions of the social workers, particularly those assumptions which are related to the essential unity of man. When the question of values comes up, as it is bound to do in counselling in whatsoever setting it occurs, then philosophy or religion are the final arbiters.

It was within the field of values that pastoral counselling was confined in the past. Hence its close connection with the work of the ordained minister and with religion. All behaviour was regarded as overt and so governed by the standards and values which were customary in the group to which the person belonged. The pastor was the authority on how people should behave, and so it fell to him to 'counsel' those who came or were brought to him, and he did so on lines recommended by ethical knowledge and the customs of the community.

But when the study of psychology revealed the importance of the unconscious part of man's behaviour, theology and philosophy could no longer claim the whole of pastoral counselling. The 'cure of souls' by psychotherapy was asserted and this seemed to by-pass the clergy who thus far had a monopoly of this form of work. It was only as they realised that the psychotherapist and the psychoanalyst were seeking to do a very similar thing to what they were trying to do that some connection between these approaches became possible.

Very much the same thing happened with social casework which has also been influenced by the new discoveries in psychology. Social casework began to be affected by the analytic approach of psychoanalysis. The awkward human adult was explained in terms of upbringing, particularly his early personal relations. He might have been a child deprived of maternal security or one who hated his father in the way which the analysts called the Oedipus complex. This has been modified in recent years to take into account the dynamic concepts of the growth of individuals in human relationships and the influence of the existing complex social situation. The influence of the unconscious is still realised but is modified by situational factors and by the many and varied interrelationships with which every person is involved.

Pastoral counselling is going through a very similar process. It too is affected by the psychological developments and by the principles which social casework has developed. To some extent it is being pulled in two different directions. On the one hand there is the clinical approach to pastoral counselling which is person-centred and which interprets behaviour largely in terms of medical science. On the other hand there is the approach of social casework, which while taking these things into account, does concern itself to a far greater extent with social and environmental factors.

The problem at the moment is to find some sort of synthesis between these two approaches. The clinical approach is particularly useful for those who are dealing with the physically or mentally ill or who are involved with people who have problems of personality, neurotic traits or stress reactions. It can be of great use when helping people who have had treatment in a mental hospital and are finding difficulties with their family or at work.

The social casework approach is more suited for the ordinary run of people whose problems may be complex and difficult but not very deep, and who do not need any psychiatric treatment. Social caseworkers have found for many years that although their methods do not command by any means a complete success, their clients feel able to give vent to their feelings with them and so find relief, or they are able to help their clients to understand what underlies the presenting problem and so to work out some solution. This may mean disclosing unsuspected anger or aggression, or revealing that some relationship is destructive and so will call for dissolution. But it will not mean digging into the depths of the personality or the unconscious mind.

The Americans have tried to solve this difficulty by making a clear distinction between counselling and clinical therapy, the former being almost entirely on a conscious level, and the latter being far deeper and needing a medical-related training. The danger which exists in this country is that of seeking to apply a medical approach to those who are not sick, and of thinking that psychiatric reasons are responsible for forms of action which have a quite simple social explanation. If it were possible to develop pastoral counselling on the lines of social casework for the vast majority of cases, those in need of deeper help could find it from the clinically trained.

A large part of counselling is supportive, that is it involves helping the person to talk freely and express his feelings. The counsellor is called upon to try to understand these feelings and behaviour in a sympathetic manner, show an interest and desire to help, express confidence that a way can be found and that the person will be able to discover this, and encourage attitudes which will enable the person to function more realistically as well as comfortably. This form of counselling is particularly valuable in helping with the everyday problems of life, for it offers a prop at a time when a person feels he is unable to cope, and so makes it more possible for him to adjust himself to the conditions of an ordinary person once more.

Counselling may need to go deeper than this to help a person not only to express but to understand his feelings, attitudes and behaviour towards those with whom he works and lives. It should enable him to see more clearly his various roles and commitments and to clarify his attitudes to them. It should also make it possible for him to think more clearly, to react more realistically and to plan more wisely. Both these aspects of counselling may be necessary in the total counselling programme, though quite often the first may be needed without any recourse to the second.

Both these levels of counselling require the sort of knowledge that has been suggested in this book and with a certain amount of study and experience the counsellor should be able to help such people satisfactorily. But when it is necessary to reach down to the unconscious and to discover motives and attitudes which the person is quite unable to bring to the surface himself then the counsellor should beware. Some clinical knowledge may help him to see that this is the case, and may even give him some idea as to what is wrong, but he is rarely in a position to do anything about it himself and should refer the person to someone who is medically qualified to deal with the needs of the patient.

It is the spiritual aspect which is the distinguishing feature of counselling that is pastoral and which brings a parting of the ways with some counsellors in the medical and social work professions. This need not be so if what the psychoanalyst and social worker mean by acceptance and empathy is what the Christian understands by love. But pastoral counselling is usually more definite than this and tries to bring about an improvement in relationships not only with other people, but with God. It works on the assumption that healing, or the process of reaching wholeness, is helped both by the methods of counselling, and by making it possible for the person to receive more fully the grace of God.

At this point it is not words so much as character which speaks. The successful counsellor is the one who can show in himself the spiritual values and attitudes which he has been commending. He needs to combine his knowledge of counselling with an acquaintance of the ultimate reality of things, and to have himself reached a relationship with God, which is secure, deep and expanding. However easily he is able to understand the feelings of the person he is counselling, however advanced his knowledge of counselling techniques may be and however well he is able to apply them, the person he is counselling will never approach complete wholeness or integration if the counsellor is unable to convey the spiritual dimension. Pastoral counselling is as much dependent upon prayer and meditation as it is upon a knowledge of the methods and principles of counselling.

References

1. M. Alan Alcock, 'What is Counselling?' in *Marriage Guidance*, Jan. 1967.
2. Quoted by Gote Bergsten, *Pastoral Psychology*, Allen & Unwin, 1951, p. 36.
3. Talcott Parsons, *The Social System*, Routledge & Kegan Paul, 1952, p. 445.
4. John Oman, *Grace and Personality*, Cambridge University Press, 1925, p. 80.
5. John Macmurray, *Reason and Emotion*, Faber & Faber, 1935, pp. 97-8.
6. Felix P. Biestek, *The Casework Relationship*, Unwin, 1961, p. 137.
7. John N. Grou, *Manual for Interior Souls*, Burns & Oates, 1955, p. 3.
8. C. G. Jung, *The Practice of Psychotherapy*, Kegan Paul, 1929, p. 55.
9. Donald D. Evans, 'Pastoral Counselling and Traditional Theology' in the *Scottish Journal of Theology*, XI:2. p. 172.

Bibliography

GENERAL

Michael Argyle, *Religious Behaviour*, Routledge & Kegan Paul, London, 1958.

W. L. Carrington, *Psychology, Religion and Human Need*, Epworth, London, 1957.

Howard J. Clinebell, *Basic Types of Pastoral Counseling*, Abingdon Press, Nashville, 1966.

Alex Comfort, *Sex in Society*, Pelican, Harmondsworth, 1964.

Frederick Greeves, *Theology and the Care of Souls*, Epworth, London, 1960.

H. Guntrip, *Psychology for Ministers and Social Workers*, Independent Press, London, 1949.

Jean Heywood, *Casework and Pastoral Care*, S.P.C.K., London, 1967.

Paul E. Johnson, *Pastoral Ministration*, Nisbet, Welwyn, 1955.

Charles Duell Kean, *Christian Faith and Pastoral Care*, S.P.C.K., London, 1961.

Philip Mairet (ed.), *Christian Essays in Psychiatry*, S.C.M., London, 1956.

G. Stephen Spinks, *Psychology and Religion*, Methuen, London, 1963.

Leslie D. Weatherhead, *Psychology, Religion and Healing*, Hodder & Stoughton, London, 1951.

CHAPTER I. SOCIETY AND COUNSELLING

H. Balmforth, L. Dewar & C. Hudson, *An Introduction to Pastoral Theology*, Hodder & Stoughton, London, 1937.

Hare Duke, *The Work of the Clinical Theology Association in Great Britain*, 1964.

Paul Halmos, *The Faith of the Counsellors*, Constable, London, 1965.

Seward Hiltner, *Preface to Pastoral Theology*, Abingdon, Nashville, 1958.

John McNeil, *A History of the Cure of Souls*, S.C.M., London, 1952.

CHAPTER II. PERSONS IN RELATIONSHIP

Gordon W. Allport, *Becoming*, Yale University Press, 1955.
Theodor Bovet, *That They May Have Life*, Darton, Longman & Todd, London, 1964.
Martin Buber, *Between Man and Man*, Fontana, London, 1966.
Martin Buber, *I and Thou* (English translation by Ronald Gregor Smith), T. & T. Clark, Edinburgh, 1937.
Dorothy M. Emmet, *Rules, Roles and Relations*, Macmillan, London, 1966.
John Macmurray, *Persons in Relation*, Faber & Faber, London, 1961.
John Macmurray, *Reason and Emotion*, Faber & Faber, London, 1935.
J. Oman, *Grace and Personality*, Cambridge University Press, London, 1925.
Carl Rogers, *On Becoming a Person*, Constable, London, 1961.
Paul Tournier, *The Meaning of Persons*, S.C.M., London, 1957.

CHAPTER III. A NEW UNDERSTANDING OF PEOPLE

Gote Bergsten, *Pastoral Psychology*, Allen & Unwin, London, 1951.
J. A. C. Brown, *Freud and the Post-Freudians*, Pelican, Harmondsworth, 1961.
Karen Horney, *The Neurotic Personality of Our Times*, Routledge & Kegan Paul, London, 1937.
Karen Horney, *Our Inner Conflicts*, Routledge & Kegan Paul, London, 1948.
Raymond Hostie, *Religion and the Psychology of Jung*, Sheed & Ward, London, 1957.
C. G. Jung, *Modern Man in Search of a Soul*, Routledge & Kegan Paul, London, 1933.
C. G. Jung, *Psychological Types*, Kegan Paul, London, 1923.
Ralph Linton, *The Cultural Background of Personality*, Routledge & Kegan Paul, London, 1947.
Ian Suttie, *The Origins of Love and Hate*, Kegan Paul, London, 1935.
Victor White, *God and the Unconscious*, Fontana, London, 1960.

CHAPTER IV. THE BASIC PRINCIPLES OF COUNSELLING

Michael Argyle, *The Psychology of Interpersonal Behaviour*, Pelican, Harmondsworth, 1967.
Felix P. Biestek, *The Casework Relationship*, Allen & Unwin, London, 1961.

Margaret Ferard & Noel Hunnybun, *The Caseworker's Use of Relationship*, Tavistock, London, 1962.
H. J. Parad & R. R. Miller (ed.), *Ego-Orientated Casework*, Family Service Association of America, 1963.
Carl Rogers, *Client-Centred Therapy*, Houghton Mifflin, Boston, 1959.
Noel Timms, *Social Casework*, Routledge & Kegan Paul, London, 1964.
J. H. Wallis, *Counselling and Social Welfare*, Routledge & Kegan Paul, London, 1960.

CHAPTER V. COUNSELLING IN ACTION

Russell L. Dick, *Principles and Practices of Pastoral Care*, Fortress Press, Philadelphia, 1963.
Annette Garrett, *Interviewing, Its Principles and Methods*, Family Service Association of America, 1942.
Seward Hiltner, *Pastoral Counseling*, Abingdon, Nashville, 1949.
Raymond Hostie, *Pastoral Counselling*, Sheed & Ward, London, 1966.
Paul E. Johnson, *Person and Counselor*, Abingdon, Nashville, 1967.
R. S. Lee, *Principles of Pastoral Counselling*, S.P.C.K., London, 1968.
C. L. Mitton (ed.), *First Aid in Counselling*, T. & T. Clark, Edinburgh, 1968.
Carl L. Rogers, *Counseling and Psychotherapy*, Constable, London, 1942.
Elizabeth & Karl de Schweinitz, *Interviewing in the Social Services*, National Institute for Social Work Training, 1962.
Carroll A. Wise, *Pastoral Counseling*, Harper Bros, New York, 1951.

CHAPTER VI. THE PASTORAL COUNSELLOR

André Godin, *The Pastoral Counsellor*, Gill & Son, Dublin, 1965.
Seward Hiltner, *The Counselor in Counseling*, Abingdon, Nashville, 1952.
William E. Hulme, *Counseling and Theology*, Muhlenberg Press, Philadelphia, 1956.
Paul Tournier, *Guilt and Grace*, Hodder & Stoughton, London, 1962.

CHAPTER VII. THE STAGES OF THE HUMAN LIFE SPAN

Counselling in Schools, Schools Council, Working Paper no. 15, 1967.
C. G. Jung, *Integration of the Personality*, Kegan Paul, London, 1944.
Margaret Moran, *Pastoral Counselling for the Deprived Girl*, Chapman, London, 1968.

F. H. Pedley (ed.), *Education and Social Welfare,* Pergamon, Oxford, 1967.
T. A. Ratcliffe, *The Development of Personality,* Allen & Unwin, London, 1967.
H. P. Steer, *Caring for the Elderly,* S.P.C.K., London, 1966.
Alfred Torrie, *The Middle Aged Man,* Church Information Office, 1959.
A. L. Vischer, *On Growing Old,* Allen & Unwin, London, 1966.
J. H. Wallis, *The Challenge of Middle Age,* Routledge & Kegan Paul, London, 1962.
Ferdinand Zweig, *The Student in the Age of Anxiety,* Heinemann, London, 1963.

CHAPTER VIII. COUNSELLING AND HEALING

Norman Autton, *Pastoral Care in Hospitals,* S.P.C.K., London, 1967.
Norman Autton, *The Pastoral Care of the Mentally Ill,* S.P.C.K., London, 1963.
J. Gordon Cox, *A Priest's Work in Hospital,* S.P.C.K., London, 1959.
Edgar Draper, *Psychiatry and Pastoral Care,* Fortress Press, Philadelphia, 1965.
Drug Dependence in Britain, Church Information Office, 1967.
E. N. Ducker, *Christian Therapy for a Neurotic World,* Allen & Unwin, London, 1961.
A. H. Purcell Fox, *The Christian Ministry of Healing,* Longmans, London, 1959.
Phyllis Garlick, *Man's Search for Health,* Highway Press, London, 1952.
Lyn Gillis, *Human Behaviour in Illness,* Faber & Faber, London, 1962.
A. Graham Ikin, *New Concepts of Healing,* Hodder & Stoughton, London, 1955.
Neil Kessel & Henry Walton, *Alcoholism,* Pelican, Harmondsworth, 1965.
R. D. Laing, *The Divided Self,* Pelican, Harmondsworth, 1965.
R. D. Laing, *The Self and Others,* Tavistock, London, 1961.
Frank Lake, *Clinical Theology,* Darton, Longman & Todd, London, 1966.
R. A. Lambourne, *Community, Church and Healing,* Darton, Longman & Todd, London, 1963.
Peter Laurie, *Drugs,* Penguin, Harmondsworth, 1967.
Loneliness, National Council of Social Service, 1964.

Chad Varah, *The Samaritans*, Constable, London, 1965.
Antony J. Wood, *Drug Dependence*, Bristol Council of Social Service, 1967.
Bertram E. Woods, *The Healing Ministry*, Rider, London, 1961.
Henry Yellowlees, *To Define True Madness*, Sidgwick & Jackson, London, 1953.

CHAPTER XI. COUNSELLING IN GROUPS

W. R. Bion, *Experience in Groups*, Tavistock, London, 1961.
John L. Casteel (ed.), *The Creative Role of Interpersonal Groups in the Church Today*, Association Press, New York, 1967.
S. H. Foulkes & E. J. Antony, *Group Psychotherapy*, Pelican, Harmondsworth, 1957.
Josephine Klein, *The Study of Groups*, Routledge & Kegan Paul, London, 1956.
W. H. Sprott, *Human Groups*, Pelican, Harmondsworth, 1962.

PERIODICALS

Churches' Council of Healing Bulletin. Quarterly, published in London.
Contact. Journal of the Scottish Pastoral Association, the Clinical Theology Association and the Institute of Religion and Medicine. Quarterly, London.
Journal of Pastoral Care. Quarterly, published by the Council for Clinical Training, New York.
Pastoral Psychology. Monthly, published in New York.
Periodical Publications of the Guild of Pastoral Psychology, London.

Index

Acceptance, 62, 86, 101, 138
Adler, Alfred, 38
Adolescent, 123, 126, 138, 169, 202
Agoraphobia, 183
Alcohol, 51, 78, 184, 202
Alcoholics Anonymous, 189, 204
Amici, 124
Anxiety, 32, 48 ff., 79, 115, 128, 130, 142, 165, 179, 193–4, 202, 209
Approval, 101, 102
Association, 26, 40, 79

Baxter, Richard, 4
Befriending, 178 ff., 182, 187, 196
Behaviour, 11, 36, 39, 55, 79
Bereaved, 142, 167
Boisen, Anton, 5, 6
Buber, Martin, 24

Catholic Marriage Advisory Council, 135
Character, 32
Child guidance, 122
Christian, 50, 51, 97, 103, 135, 162, 183
Clarification, 86
Clergy, 1, 6, 18, 93, 120, 128, 135, 156, 166, 187, 197, 211
Clinical theology, 6, 107, 212, 214
Communication, 71, 209
Community, 30, 46, 168
Conflict, 32, 50, 80, 97, 171, 176, 193, 209

Congregation, 106, 160, 170, 178, 205
Conscience, 32, 97, 98, 99, 141
Consciousness, 40
Council for Clinical Training, 5
Counselling, Chapters IV, V
   Aim, 2, 52
   Alcoholics, 184–92
   American, 5, 6, 65, 93, 120, 122, 213
   Definition, 1
   Drug addicts, 192–7
   Elderly, 146–56
   Group, Chapter IX
   Length, 90
   Lonely, 177–83
   Marriage, 128–36
   Mentally ill, 171–6
   Methods, 1, 81, 85, 208
   Middle-aged, 137–45
   Non-directive, 6, 94, 104
   Premarital, 128–9
   Relationship, 55 ff.
   Sick, 161–70
   Spiritual, 134, 144, 145, 158, 159, 214
   Supportive, 9, 10, 206, 213
   Young, 119–28
Counsellor, 30, 60, 66, 69, 71, 74, 82, 89, 203
Cruse clubs, 168

Death, 16, 67, 97, 150, 155, 166
Depression, 152, 179, 180–2

INDEX

Divorce, 136
Doctor, 1, 15, 18, 54, 140, 164, 166, 169, 186, 188, 211
Drugs, 51, 192 ff., 202

Ego-psychology, 64, 65
Emotions, 37, 57, 60, 63, 64, 68, 74, 75, 81, 90, 113, 131, 133, 180, 200, 205
Environment, 5, 10, 21, 66, 87, 123, 147, 149, 152, 210
Evans, Donald, 103

Family, 30, 117, 119, 148, 167, 191
Family lawyer, 1, 16
Fantasy, 141, 143, 167, 173
Fear, 49, 161, 174
Freud, Sigmund, 37, 41, 59, 64, 98

Galen, 42
God, 90, 103, 104, 125, 153, 159, 190, 208, 214
Grief, 136, 167
Groups, 120, 123, 127, 156, 160, 168, 180, 189
Guilt, 98, 136, 153, 170

Halmos, Paul, 17
Handicapped, 67, 78, 123, 168, 169, 188
Healing, Chapter VIII, 214
Hiltner, Seward, 8
Homosexual, 180
Horney, Karen, 39
Hospital, 163, 168, 196, 207
Hospital chaplain, 158, 163

I-and-Thou relationship, 25, 33
Illness, 146

Infidelity, 142
Insight, 80, 82, 83, 200, 203
Instincts, 36
Interviewing, 70, 79, 85, 87, 89, 132, 188

Jung, C. G., 22, 43, 48, 103

Kretschmer, E., 42

Lake, Frank, 6, 42
Leader, 127, 199, 203, 204
Listening, 59, 73, 74, 163
Loneliness, 148, 177 ff.
Love, 61, 105, 126, 175, 214
Luther, Martin, 3

McDougall, William, 35
Macmurray, John, 27
Marriage, 116, 127, 128, 129, 133
Marriage Guidance Council, 122, 127, 129, 132, 202
Middle-age, 67, 118, 137 ff.

National Association for Mental Health, 107
Neurosis, 52, 88, 111, 153, 171
Note-taking, 90

Old age, 66, 67, 118, 146 ff.
Oman, John, 26
Open Door, 184

Parent-child relationship, 121
Parsons, Talcott, 15
Pastoral counselling, 5, 8, 15, 34, 56, 93, 158, 170

Pastoral Counselling (*cont.*)
  Directive, 94
  Eclectic, 95
  History, 2 ff., 7, 35, 212
Pastoral counsellor, Chapter VI, 7, 33, 145, 207, 215
Person, 20, 23, 25, 69
  Aspects, 22
  Equality, 28
  Façade, 21, 33
  Freedom, 28, 50
Personality development, 111 ff.
  Difficulties, 88
  Integration, 21, 31, 60, 136, 155, 162, 214
  Types, 43 ff., 54, 83, 209
Problem solution, 96
Projection, 31, 41, 49, 81, 136, 140
Psychiatry, 3, 7, 16, 37, 196, 210
Psycho-analysis, 22, 59, 211
Psychology, 82, 209, 211
Psychotherapy, 5, 6, 8, 52, 53, 81, 134, 176, 196, 211

Questions, 75, 76, 78

Relationships, 26, 28, 55, 113, 120, 208
Religious conversion, 126, 141
Repression, 41, 82, 100
Retirement, 149 ff.
Richmond Fellowship, 107
Rogers, Carl, 6
Roles, 11, 66, 92, 116, 122, 210, 213

Sacraments, 18, 105
Samaritans, 183, 184
School child, 122, 123
Security, 2, 4, 13, 31, 96, 148, 151, 206
Self-consciousness, 23
Self-determination, 63
Sex, 38, 126, 127, 128, 133, 202
Sick, 161 ff.
Sin, 101, 159
Social worker, 16, 54, 124, 166, 169, 186, 187, 197, 210, 212
Society, 1, 2, 11, 27, 50, 66, 118, 136, 139, 156, 179
Spinster, 138
Spiritual healing, 158, 159
Subnormality, 187
Suicide, 180, 182

Tavistock Institute, 108
Teacher, 1, 16, 114, 120, 122, 197
Training, 6, 106, 108
Transference, 59, 81, 133

Unconscious, 37, 40, 211

Weatherhead, Leslie, 6
Wise, Carroll, 6

Youth clubs, 115, 124, 127, 205, 206